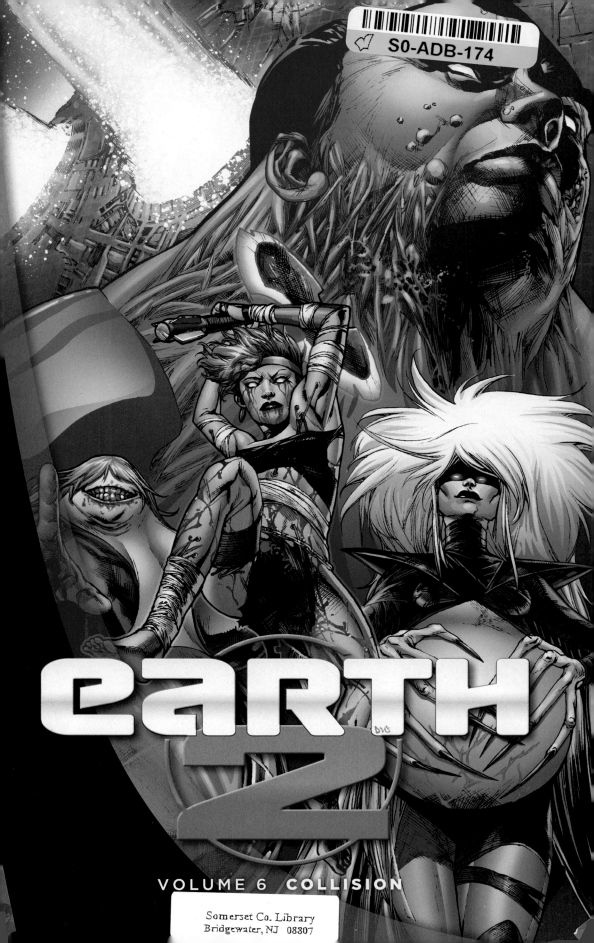

eARTH 2

VOLUME 6 COLLISION

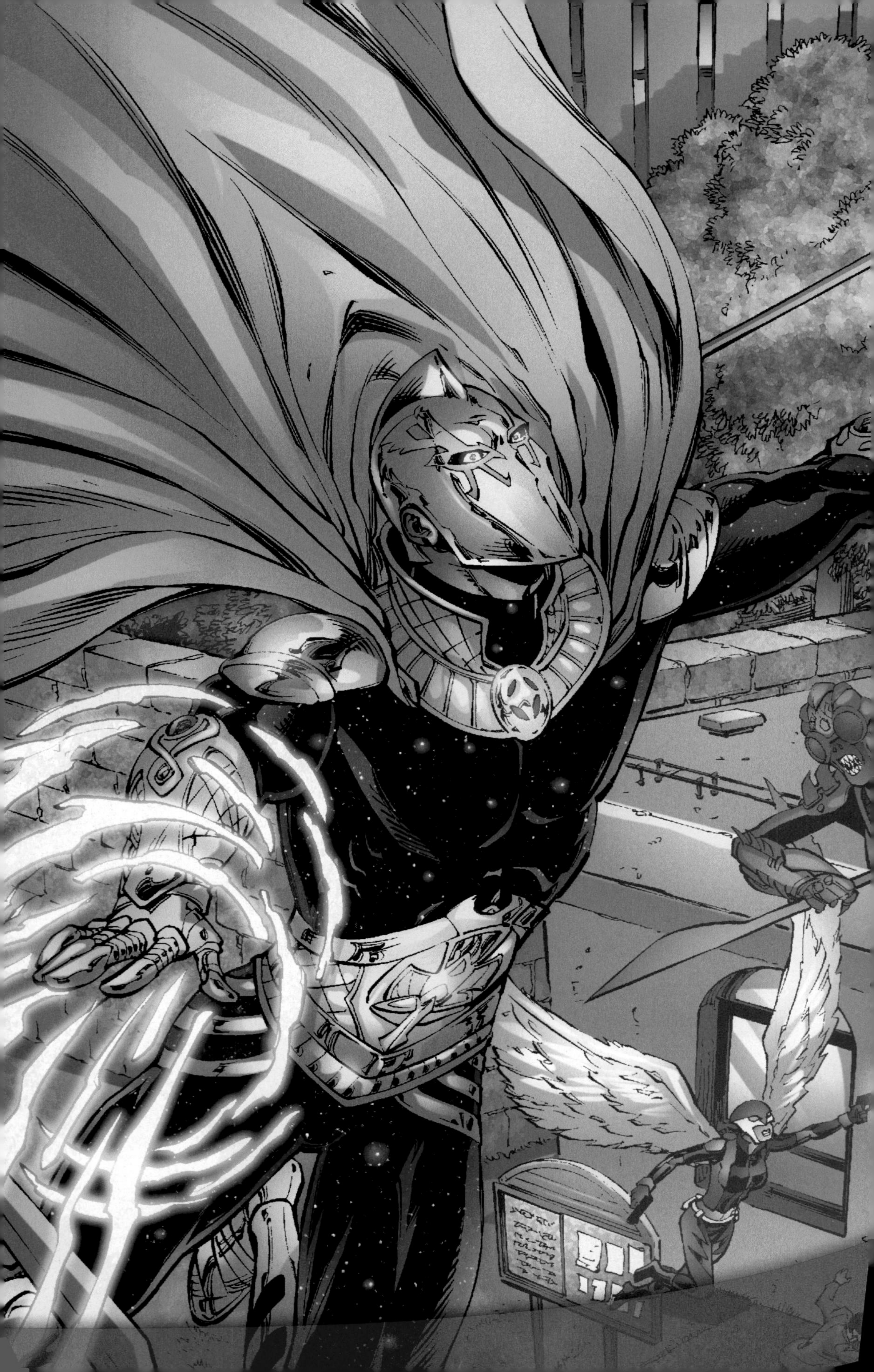

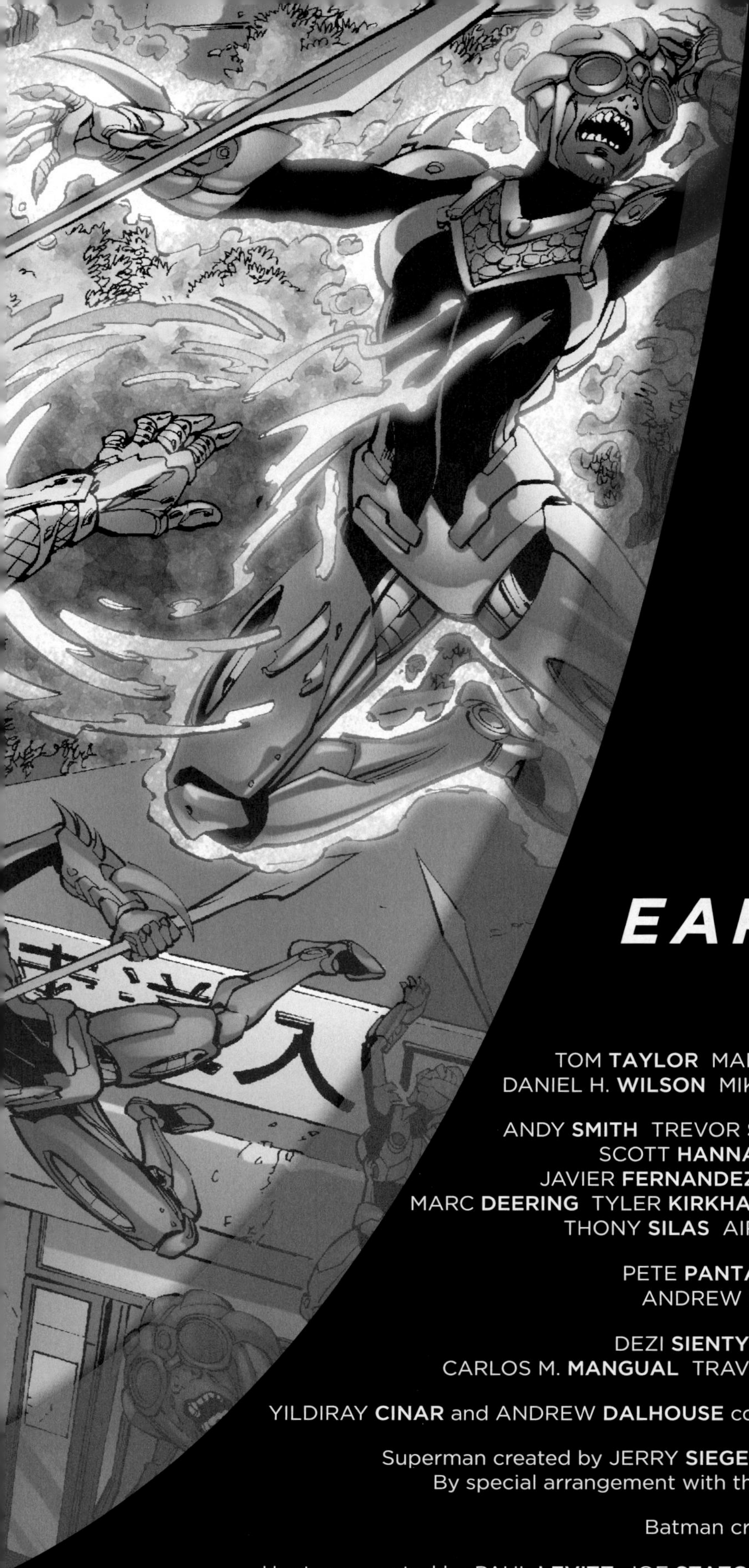

EARTH 2

VOLUME 6
COLLISION

TOM **TAYLOR** MARGUERITE **BENNETT**
DANIEL H. **WILSON** MIKE **JOHNSON** writers

ANDY **SMITH** TREVOR **SCOTT** MARCUS **TO**
SCOTT **HANNA** ALISSON **BORGES**
JAVIER **FERNANDEZ** DIOGENES **NEVES**
MARC **DEERING** TYLER **KIRKHAM** CLIFF **RICHARDS**
THONY **SILAS** AIRI **KAMIYAMA** artists

PETE **PANTAZIS** MATT **YACKEY**
ANDREW **DALHOUSE** colorists

DEZI **SIENTY** TAYLOR **ESPOSITO**
CARLOS M. **MANGUAL** TRAVIS **LANHAM** letterers

YILDIRAY **CINAR** and ANDREW **DALHOUSE** collection cover artists

Superman created by JERRY **SIEGEL** and JOE **SHUSTER**
By special arrangement with the Jerry Siegel family

Batman created by BOB **KANE**

Huntress created by PAUL **LEVITZ**, JOE **STATON** and BOB **LAYTON**

EDDIE BERGANZA MIKE COTTON Editors – Original Series RICKEY PURDIN Associate Editor – Original Series
JEREMY BENT Assistant Editor – Original Series JEB WOODARD Group Editor – Collected Editions
LIZ ERICKSON Editor – Collected Edition ROBBIE BIEDERMAN – Publication Design

BOB HARRAS Senior VP – Editor-in-Chief, DC Comics

DIANE NELSON President DAN DiDIO Publisher JIM LEE Publisher GEOFF JOHNS President & Chief Creative Officer
AMIT DESAI Executive VP – Business & Marketing Strategy, Direct to Consumer & Global Franchise Management
SAM ADES Senior VP – Direct to Consumer BOBBIE CHASE VP – Talent Development
MARK CHIARELLO Senior VP – Art, Design & Collected Editions JOHN CUNNINGHAM Senior VP – Sales & Trade Marketing
ANNE DePIES Senior VP – Business Strategy, Finance & Administration DON FALLETTI VP – Manufacturing Operations
LAWRENCE GANEM VP – Editorial Administration & Talent Relations ALISON GILL Senior VP – Manufacturing & Operations
HANK KANALZ Senior VP – Editorial Strategy & Administration JAY KOGAN VP – Legal Affairs THOMAS LOFTUS VP – Business Affairs
JACK MAHAN VP – Business Affairs NICK J. NAPOLITANO VP – Manufacturing Administration EDDIE SCANNELL VP – Consumer Marketing
COURTNEY SIMMONS Senior VP – Publicity & Communications JIM (SKI) SOKOLOWSKI VP – Comic Book Specialty & Trade Marketing
NANCY SPEARS VP – Mass, Book, Digital Sales & Trade Marketing

EARTH 2 VOLUME 6: COLLISION

DC Comics, 2900 West Alameda Ave., Burbank, CA 91505
Printed by LSC Communications, Salem, VA, USA. 1/6/17. First Printing.
ISBN: 978-1-4012-7261-6

Library of Congress Cataloging-in-Publication Data is available.

PEFC Certified
Printed on paper from sustainably managed forests, controlled sources
PEFC
PEFC/29-31-337
www.pefc.org

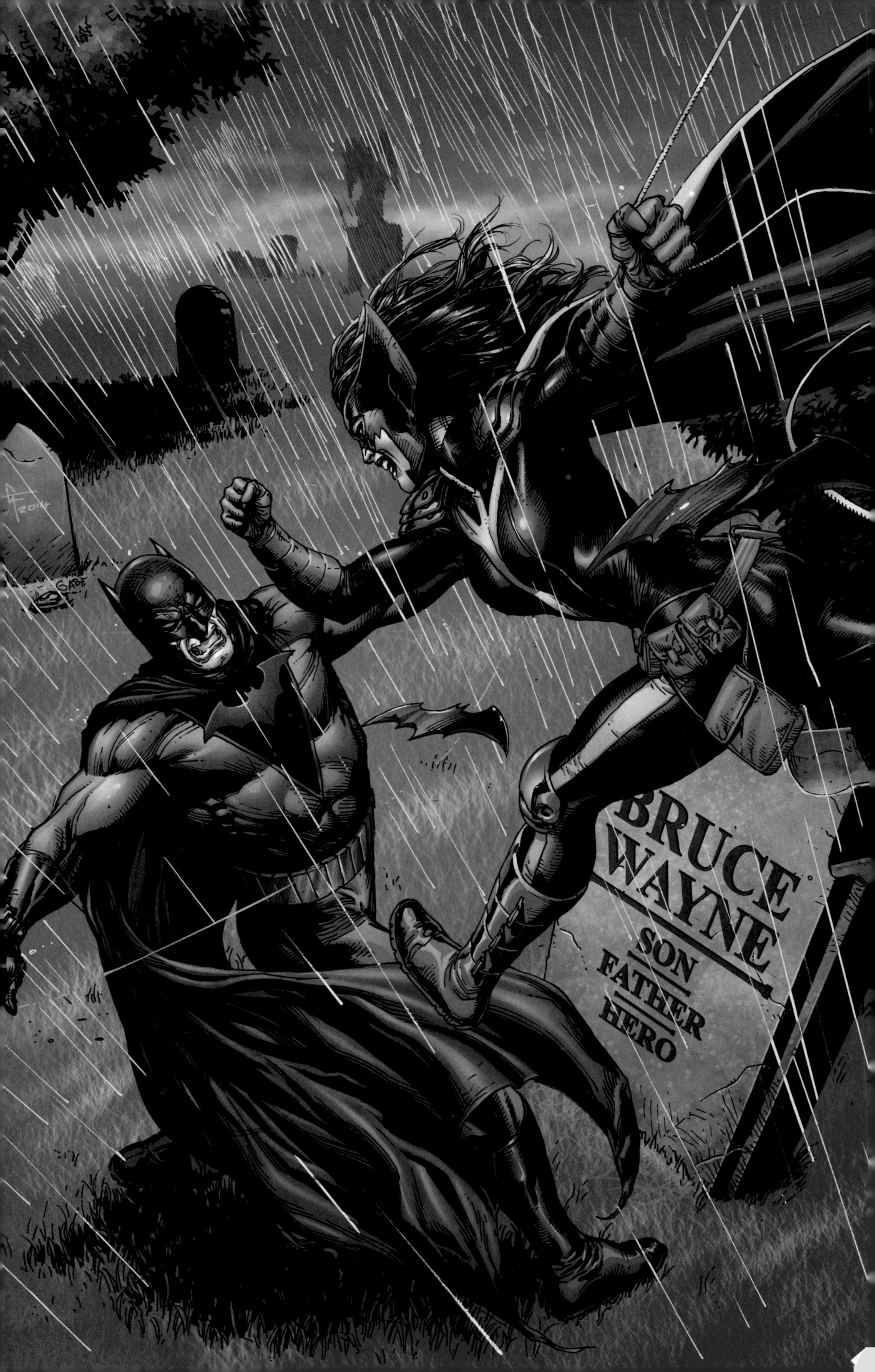

BRUCE WAYNE
SON
FATHER
HERO

COLLISION

MARGUERITE BENNETT, TOM TAYLOR writers **ANDY SMITH, TREVOR SCOTT, MARCUS TO, SCOTT HANNA** artists
PETE PANTAZIS colorist **DEZI SIENTY** letterer cover by **GARY FRANK** with **GABE ELTAEB**

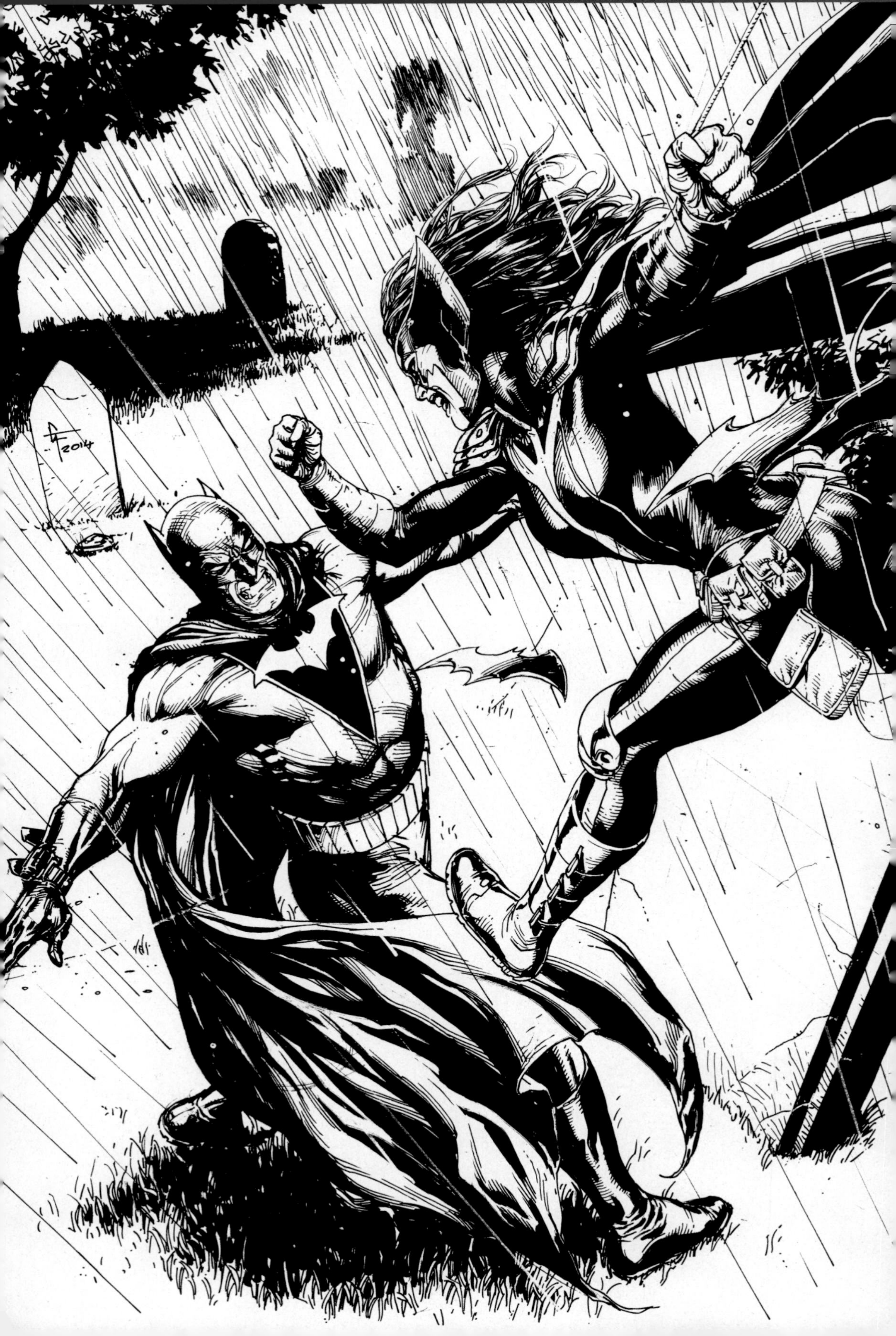

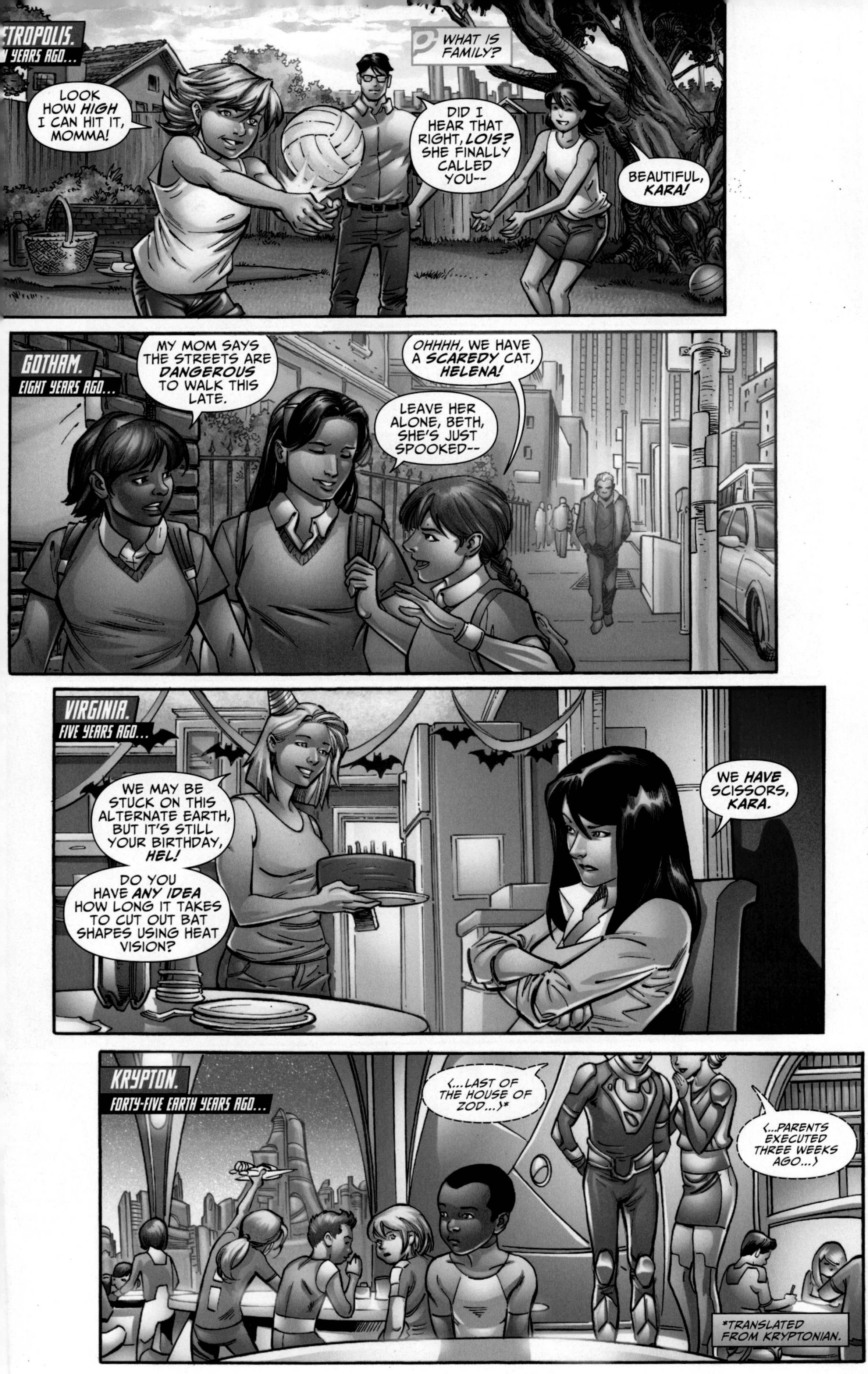

ETROPOLIS.
N YEARS AGO...
WHAT IS FAMILY?
LOOK HOW HIGH I CAN HIT IT, MOMMA!
DID I HEAR THAT RIGHT, LOIS? SHE FINALLY CALLED YOU--
BEAUTIFUL, KARA!
GOTHAM.
EIGHT YEARS AGO...
MY MOM SAYS THE STREETS ARE DANGEROUS TO WALK THIS LATE.
OHHHH, WE HAVE A SCAREDY CAT, HELENA!
LEAVE HER ALONE, BETH, SHE'S JUST SPOOKED--
VIRGINIA.
FIVE YEARS AGO...
WE MAY BE STUCK ON THIS ALTERNATE EARTH, BUT IT'S STILL YOUR BIRTHDAY, HEL!
DO YOU HAVE ANY IDEA HOW LONG IT TAKES TO CUT OUT BAT SHAPES USING HEAT VISION?
WE HAVE SCISSORS, KARA.
KRYPTON.
FORTY-FIVE EARTH YEARS AGO...
‹...LAST OF THE HOUSE OF ZOD...›*
‹...PARENTS EXECUTED THREE WEEKS AGO...›
*TRANSLATED FROM KRYPTONIAN.

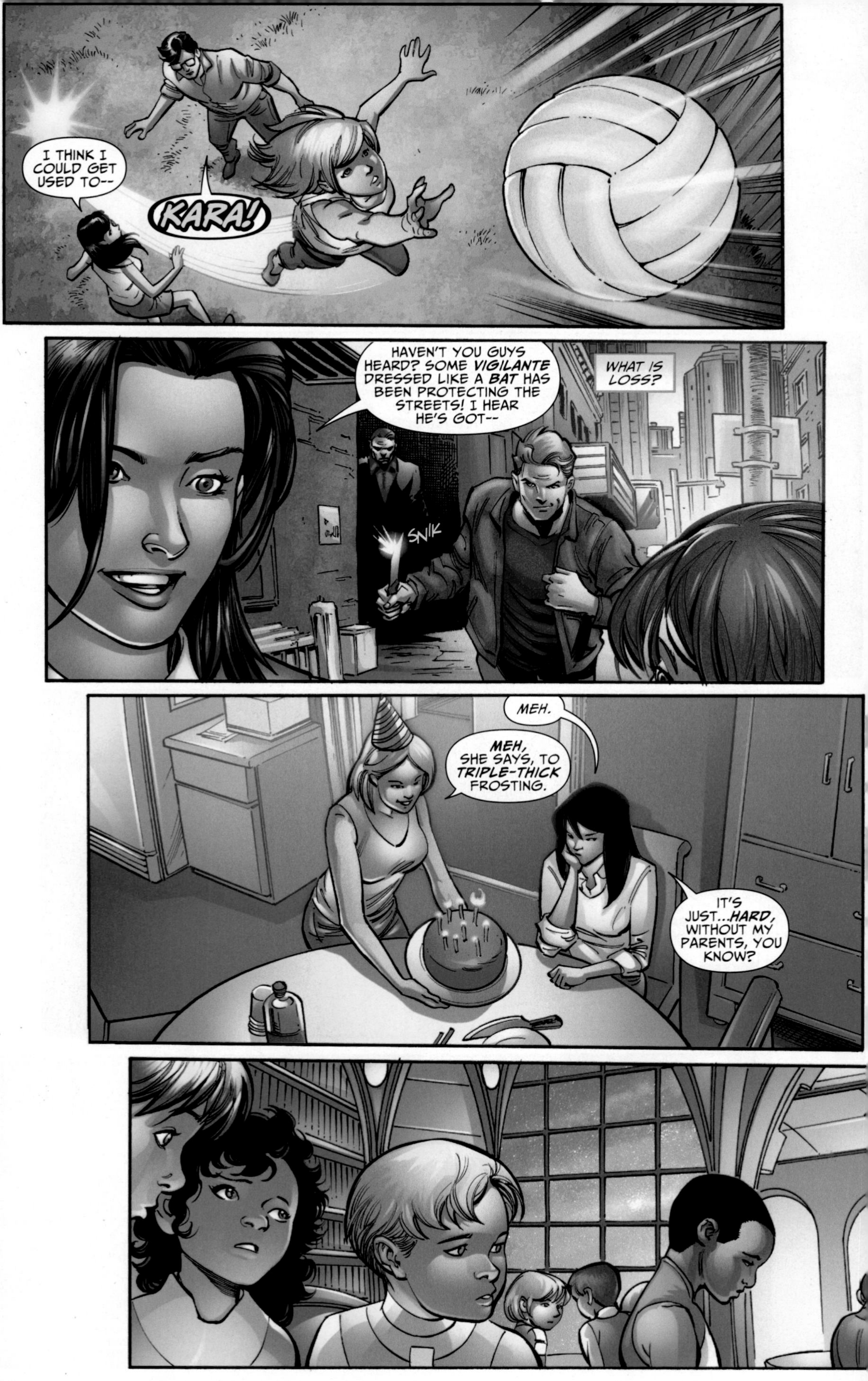
I THINK I COULD GET USED TO--
KARA!
HAVEN'T YOU GUYS HEARD? SOME *VIGILANTE* DRESSED LIKE A *BAT* HAS BEEN PROTECTING THE STREETS! I HEAR HE'S GOT--
WHAT IS LOSS?
SNIK
MEH.
MEH, SHE SAYS, TO *TRIPLE-THICK* FROSTING.
IT'S JUST...*HARD,* WITHOUT MY PARENTS, YOU KNOW?

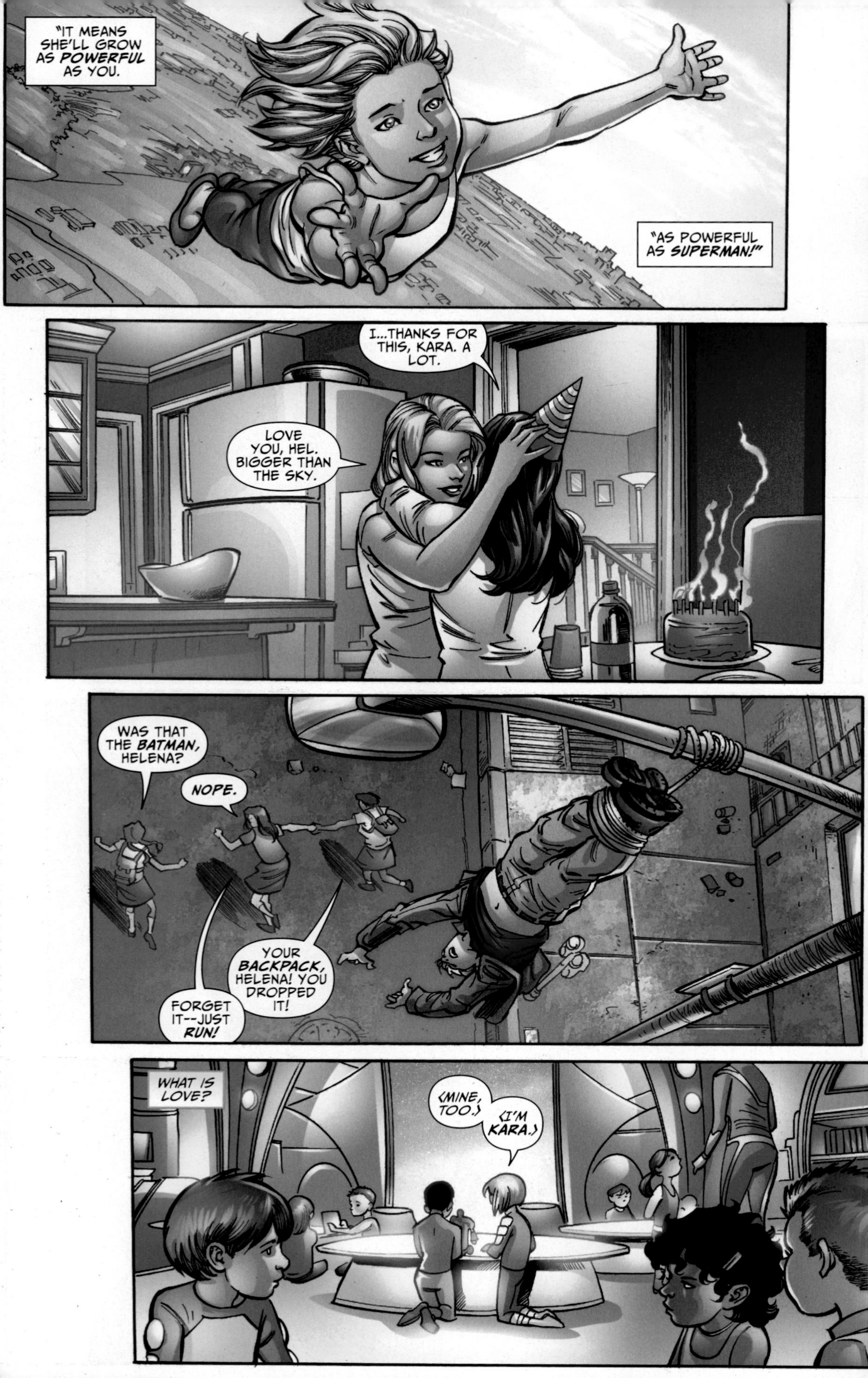
"IT MEANS SHE'LL GROW AS POWERFUL AS YOU.
"AS POWERFUL AS SUPERMAN!"
I...THANKS FOR THIS, KARA. A LOT.
LOVE YOU, HEL. BIGGER THAN THE SKY.
WAS THAT THE BATMAN, HELENA?
NOPE.
YOUR BACKPACK, HELENA! YOU DROPPED IT!
FORGET IT--JUST RUN!
WHAT IS LOVE?
‹MINE, TOO.›
‹I'M KARA.›

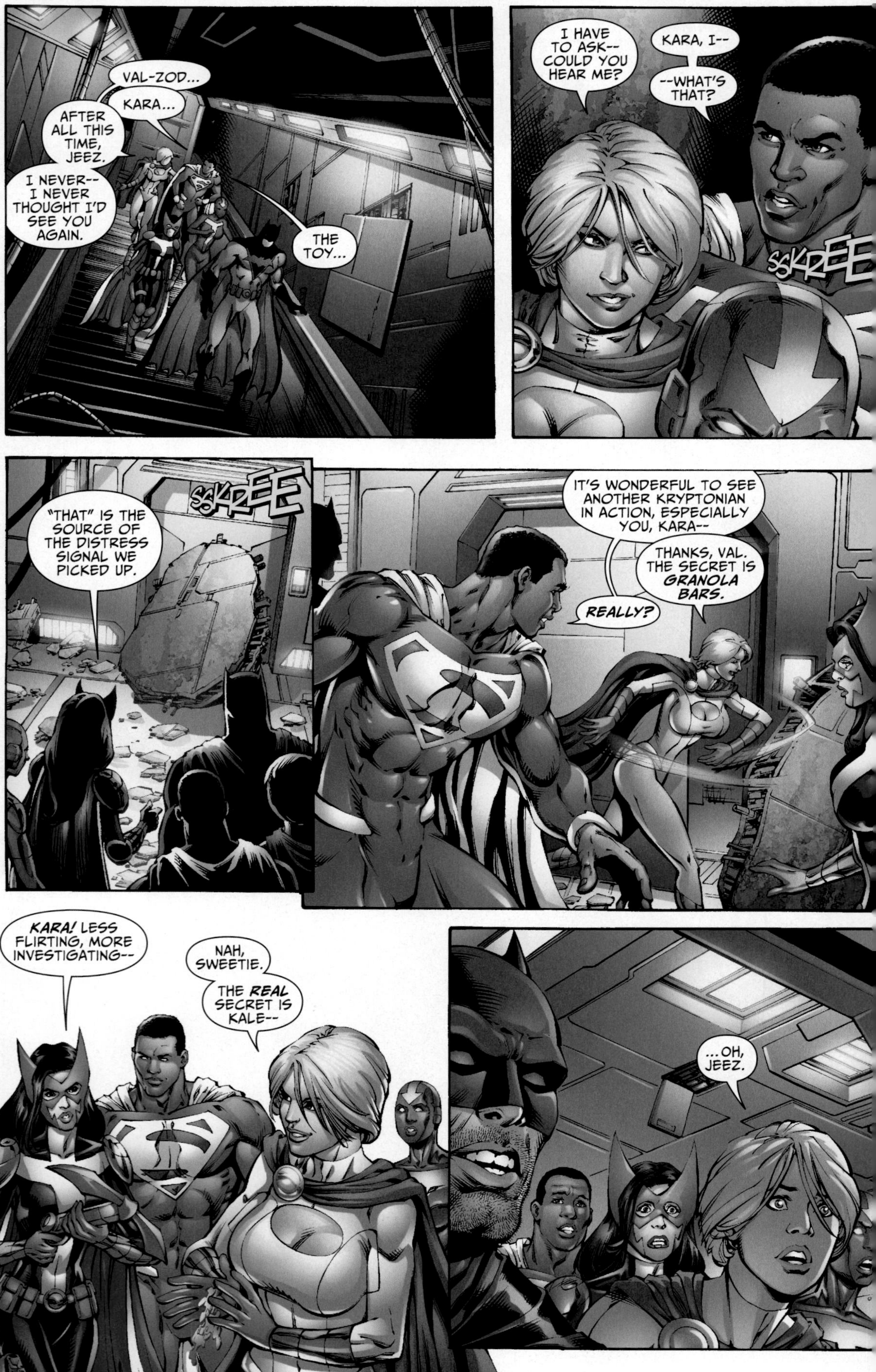
VAL-ZOD...
KARA...
AFTER ALL THIS TIME, JEEZ.
I NEVER-- I NEVER THOUGHT I'D SEE YOU AGAIN.
THE TOY...
I HAVE TO ASK-- COULD YOU HEAR ME?
KARA, I--
--WHAT'S THAT?
SSKREE
SSKREEE
"THAT" IS THE SOURCE OF THE DISTRESS SIGNAL WE PICKED UP.
IT'S WONDERFUL TO SEE ANOTHER KRYPTONIAN IN ACTION, ESPECIALLY YOU, KARA--
THANKS, VAL. THE SECRET IS GRANOLA BARS.
REALLY?
KARA! LESS FLIRTING, MORE INVESTIGATING--
NAH, SWEETIE.
THE REAL SECRET IS KALE--
...OH, JEEZ.

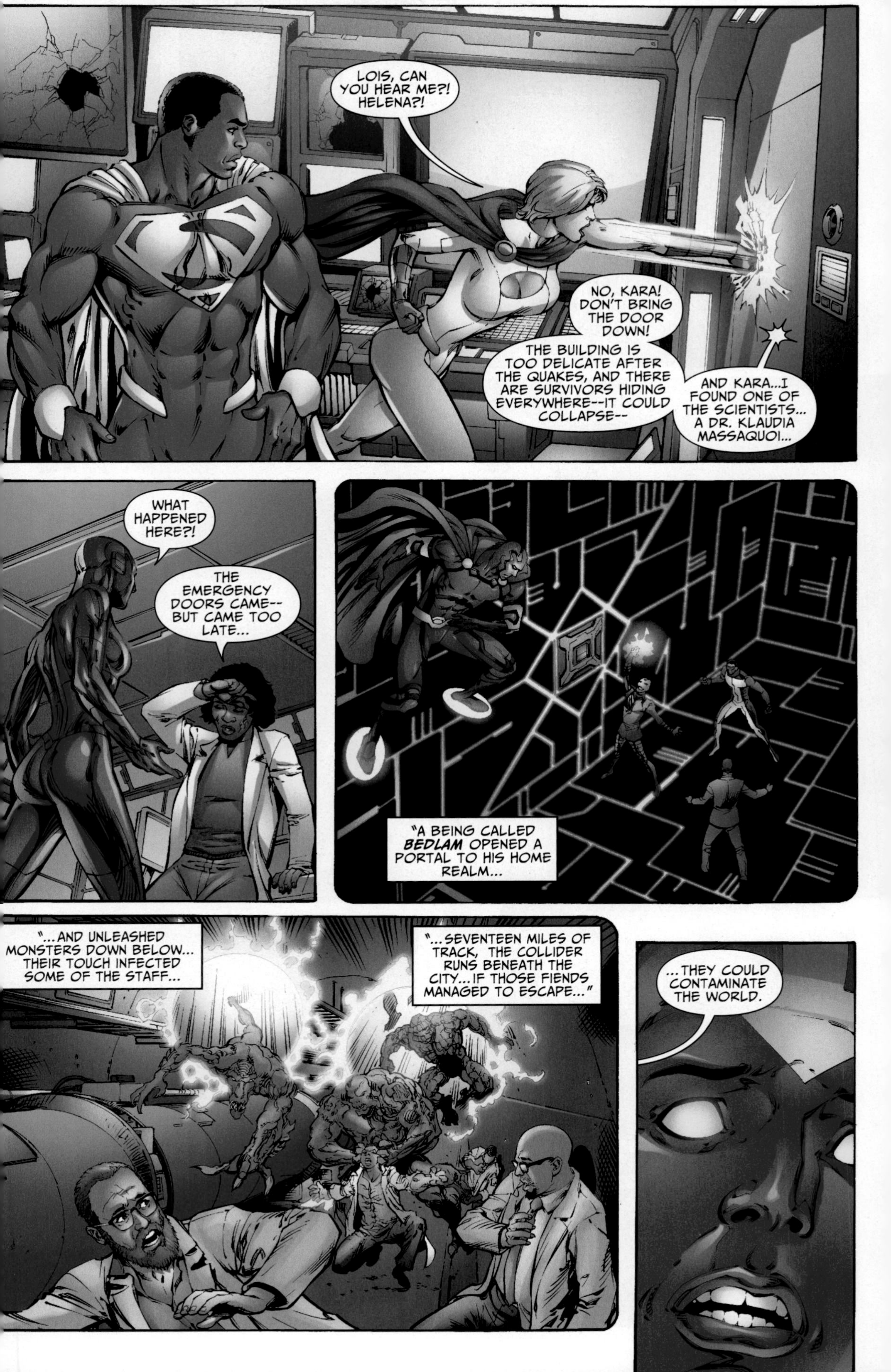
LOIS, CAN YOU HEAR ME?! HELENA?!
NO, KARA! DON'T BRING THE DOOR DOWN!
THE BUILDING IS TOO DELICATE AFTER THE QUAKES, AND THERE ARE SURVIVORS HIDING EVERYWHERE--IT COULD COLLAPSE--
AND KARA...I FOUND ONE OF THE SCIENTISTS... A DR. KLAUDIA MASSAQUOI...
WHAT HAPPENED HERE?!
THE EMERGENCY DOORS CAME--BUT CAME TOO LATE...
"A BEING CALLED BEDLAM OPENED A PORTAL TO HIS HOME REALM...
"...AND UNLEASHED MONSTERS DOWN BELOW... THEIR TOUCH INFECTED SOME OF THE STAFF...
"...SEVENTEEN MILES OF TRACK, THE COLLIDER RUNS BENEATH THE CITY...IF THOSE FIENDS MANAGED TO ESCAPE..."
...THEY COULD CONTAMINATE THE WORLD.

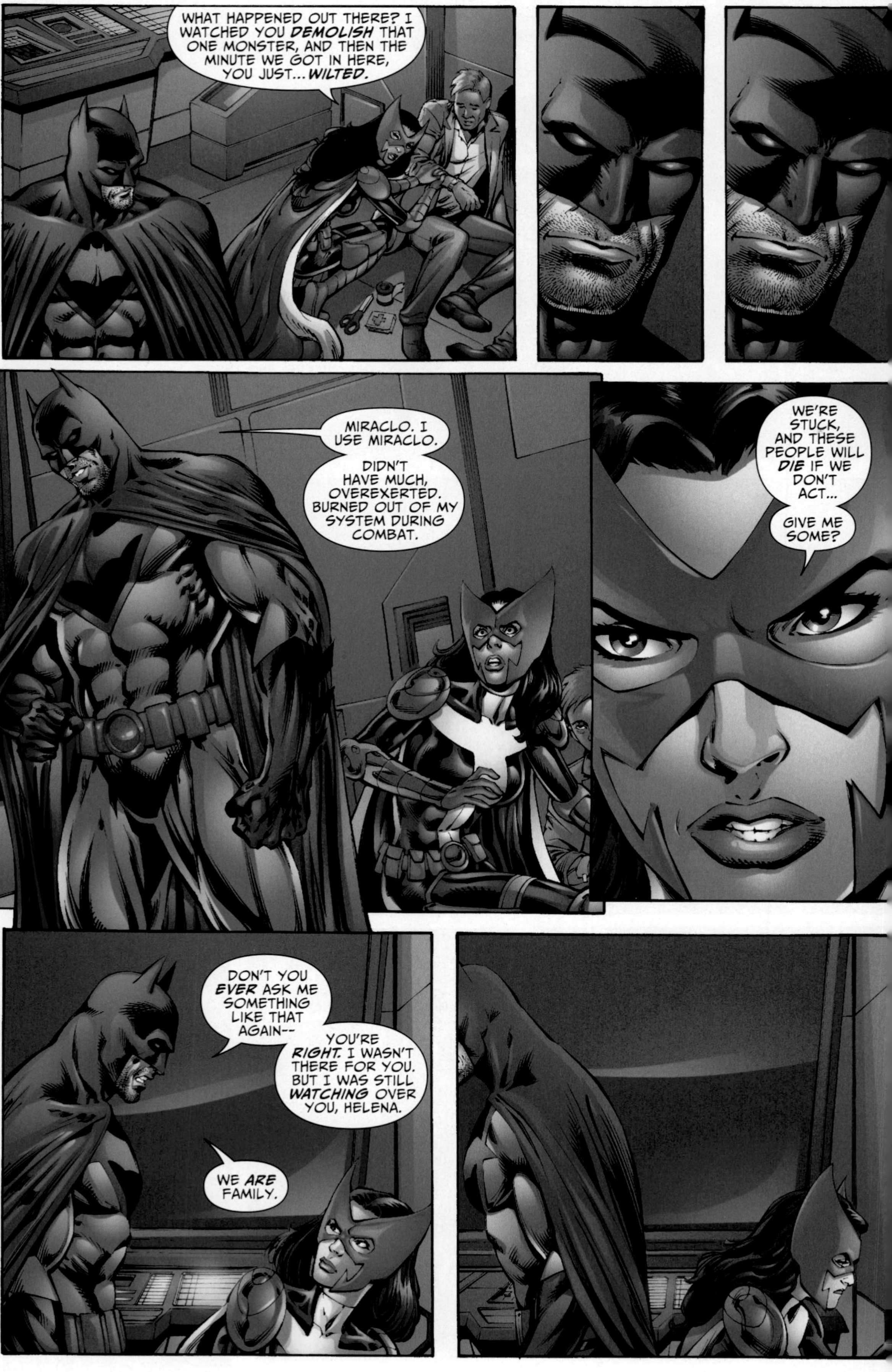
WHAT HAPPENED OUT THERE? I WATCHED YOU DEMOLISH THAT ONE MONSTER, AND THEN THE MINUTE WE GOT IN HERE, YOU JUST... WILTED.
MIRACLO. I USE MIRACLO.
DIDN'T HAVE MUCH, OVEREXERTED. BURNED OUT OF MY SYSTEM DURING COMBAT.
WE'RE STUCK, AND THESE PEOPLE WILL DIE IF WE DON'T ACT...
GIVE ME SOME?
DON'T YOU EVER ASK ME SOMETHING LIKE THAT AGAIN--
YOU'RE RIGHT. I WASN'T THERE FOR YOU. BUT I WAS STILL WATCHING OVER YOU, HELENA.
WE ARE FAMILY.

HERE, DR. ASSAQUO!...

...MY DAUGHTER AND R FRIEND CAN LP, THEY ARE RYPTONIAN--

YOUNG MAN? YOUNG MISS?

YOUNG MAN, YOU WEAR THE SYMBOL OF THE MAN OF STEEL....IT WAS SAID HE COULD REACH SUCH SPEEDS, INCALCULABLE...

K AK

...IF YOU WERE ABLE TO GENERATE SUCH A SPEED, AND COLLIDE, WITH SUCH AN EXPULSION OF ENERGY, YOU COULD CREATE AN EVENT SIMILAR TO THAT OF A NEUTRON BOMB--

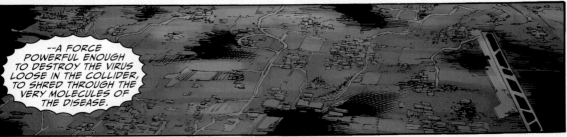

--A FORCE POWERFUL ENOUGH TO DESTROY THE VIRUS LOOSE IN THE COLLIDER, TO SHRED THROUGH THE VERY MOLECULES OF THE DISEASE.

WILL YOU RISK THIS?

WHAM

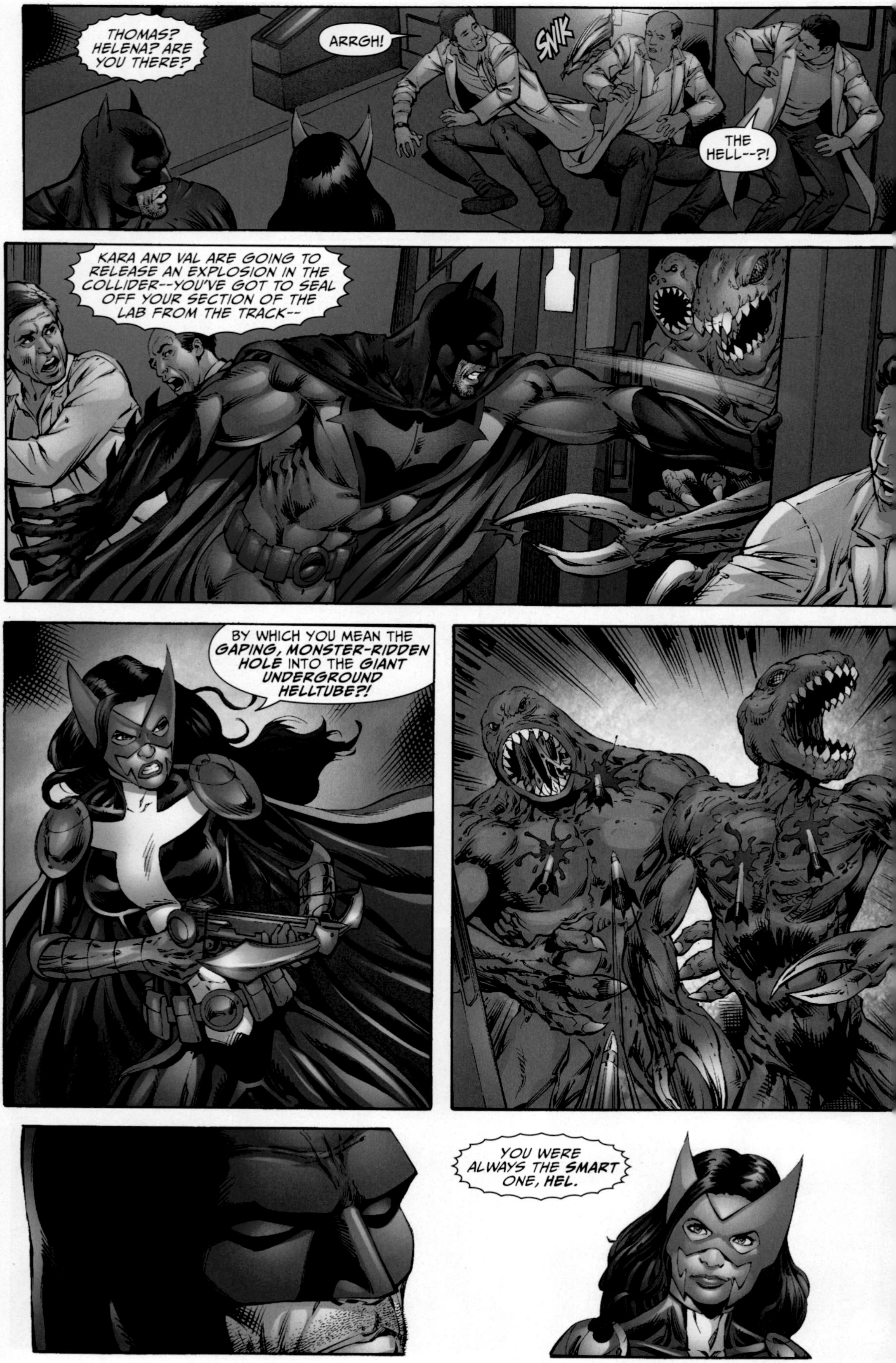
THOMAS? HELENA? ARE YOU THERE?
ARRGH!
SNIK
THE HELL--?!
KARA AND VAL ARE GOING TO RELEASE AN EXPLOSION IN THE COLLIDER--YOU'VE GOT TO SEAL OFF YOUR SECTION OF THE LAB FROM THE TRACK--
BY WHICH YOU MEAN THE GAPING, MONSTER-RIDDEN HOLE INTO THE GIANT UNDERGROUND HELLTUBE?!
YOU WERE ALWAYS THE SMART ONE, HEL.

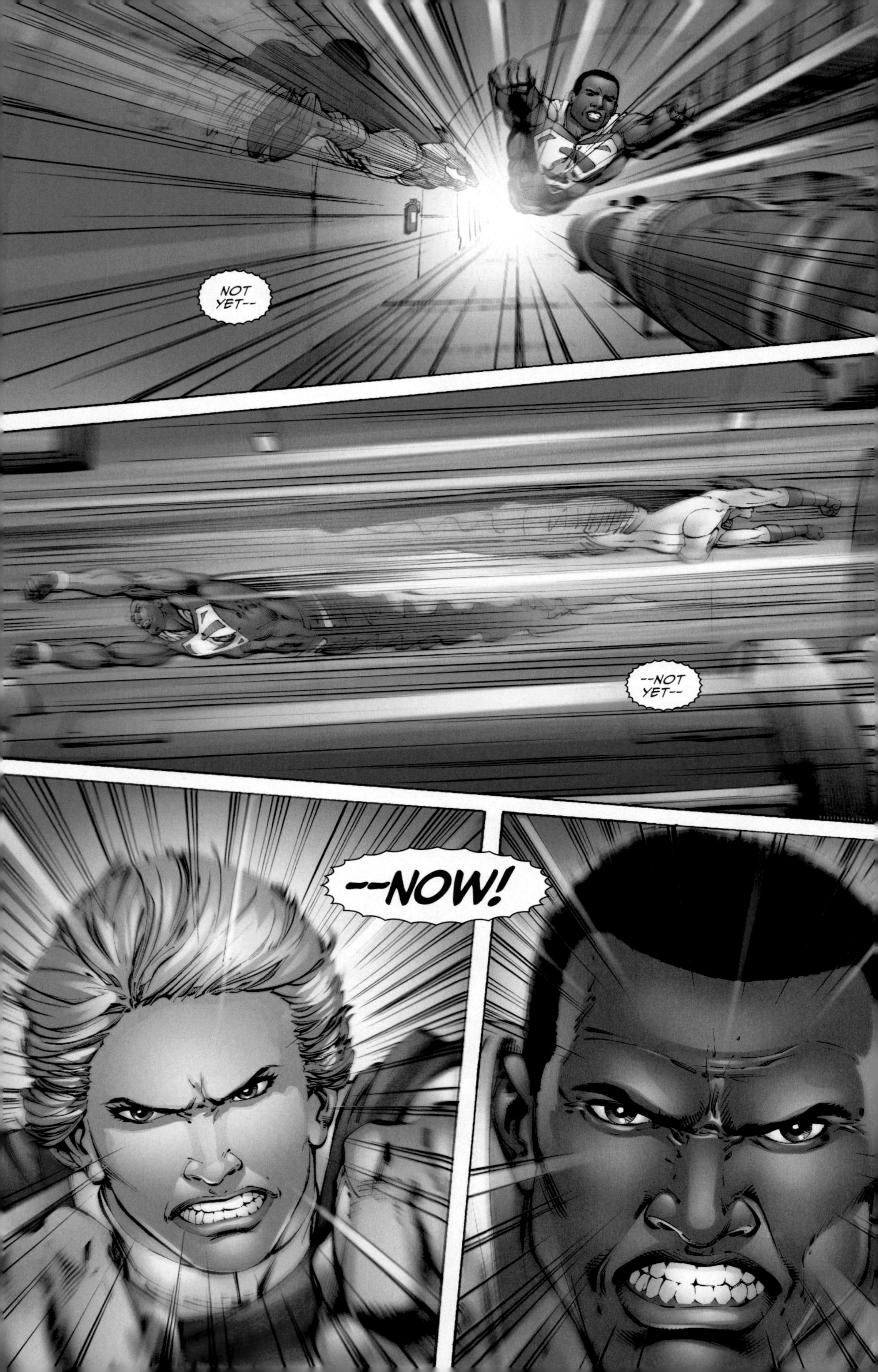
NOT YET--
--NOT YET--
--NOW!

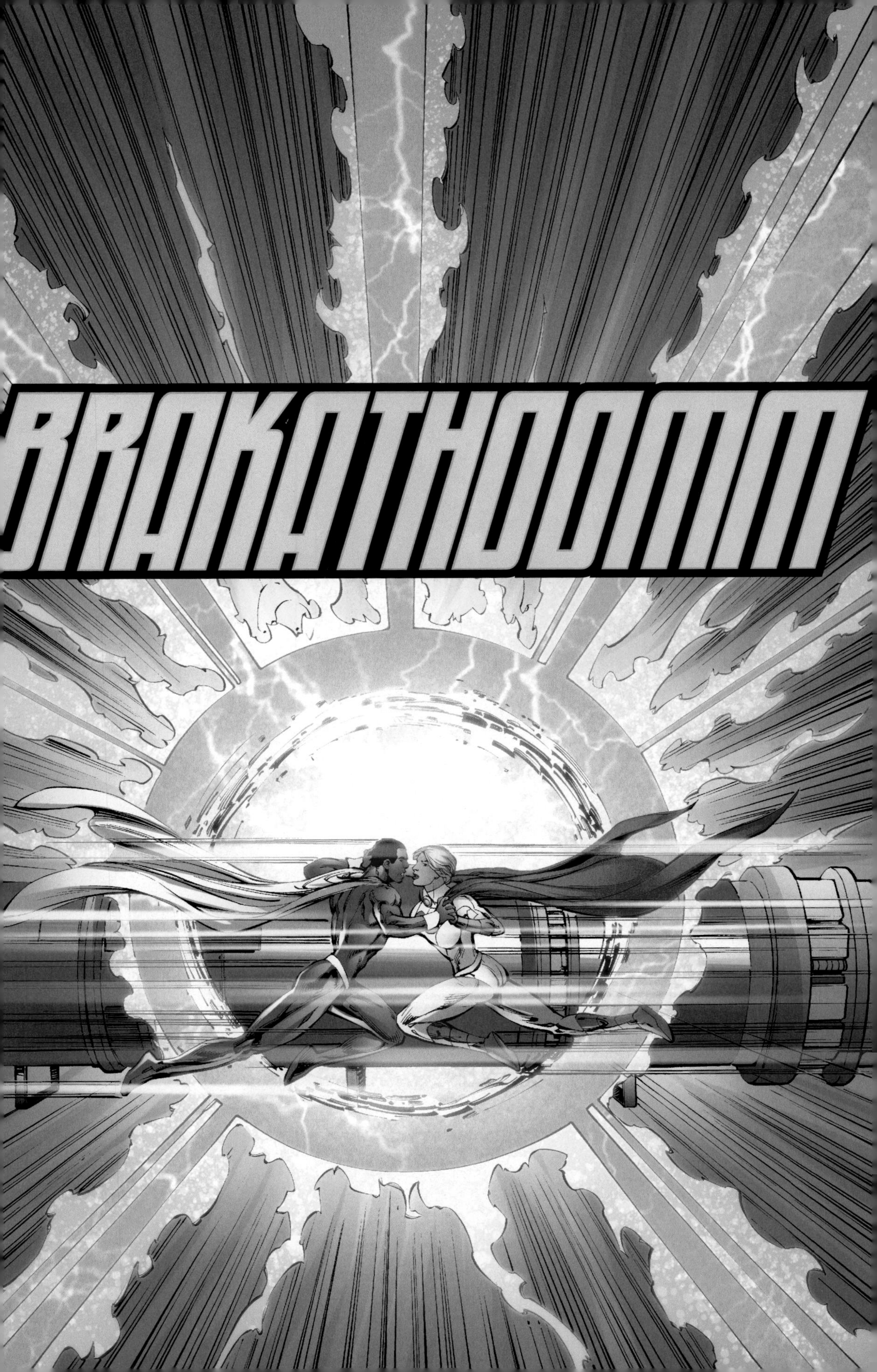
BRAKATHOOMM

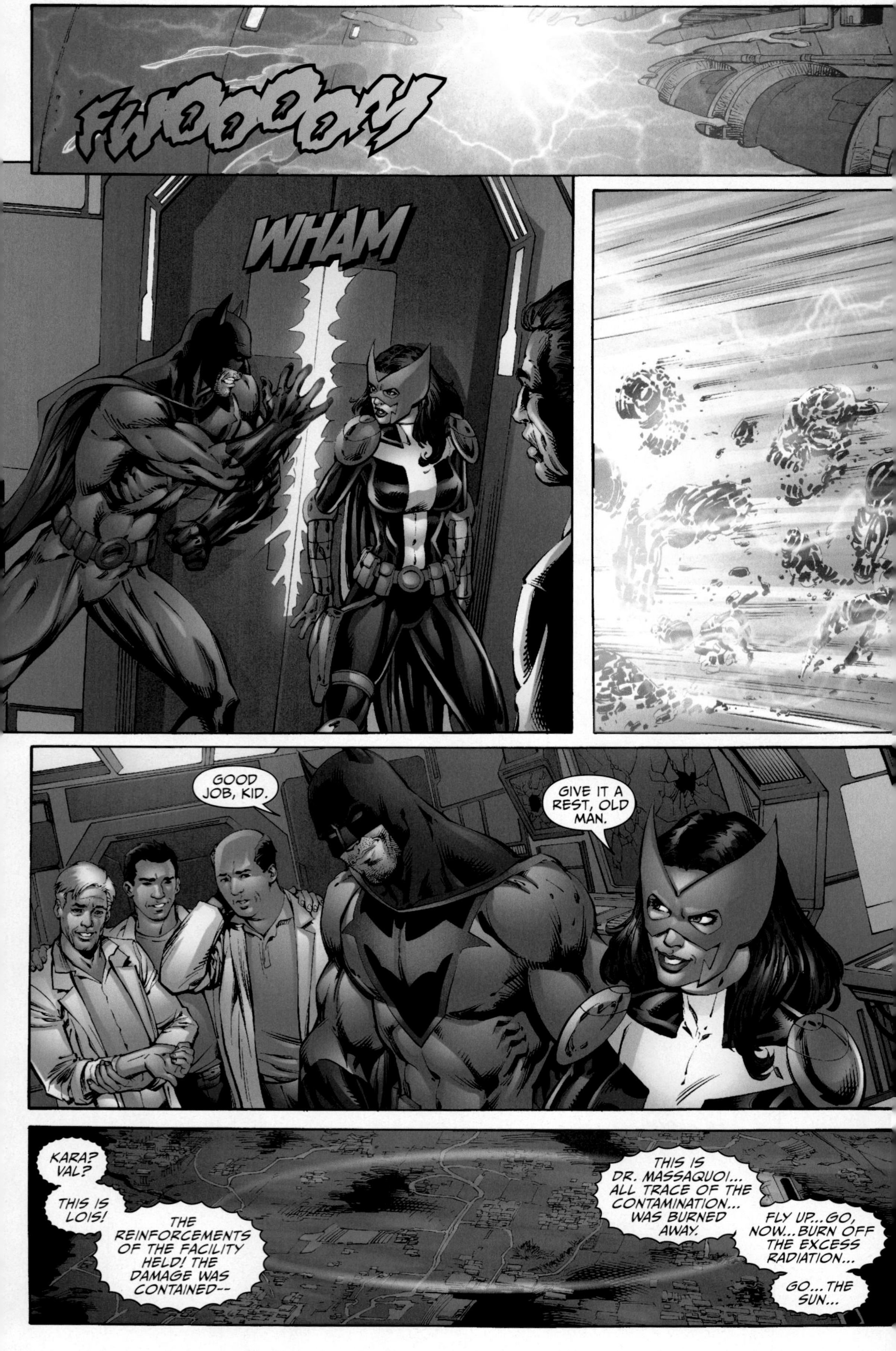
FWOOOOM
WHAM
GOOD JOB, KID.
GIVE IT A REST, OLD MAN.
KARA? VAL?
THIS IS LOIS!
THE REINFORCEMENTS OF THE FACILITY HELD! THE DAMAGE WAS CONTAINED--
THIS IS DR. MASSAQUOI... ALL TRACE OF THE CONTAMINATION... WAS BURNED AWAY.
FLY UP...GO, NOW...BURN OFF THE EXCESS RADIATION...
GO... THE SUN...

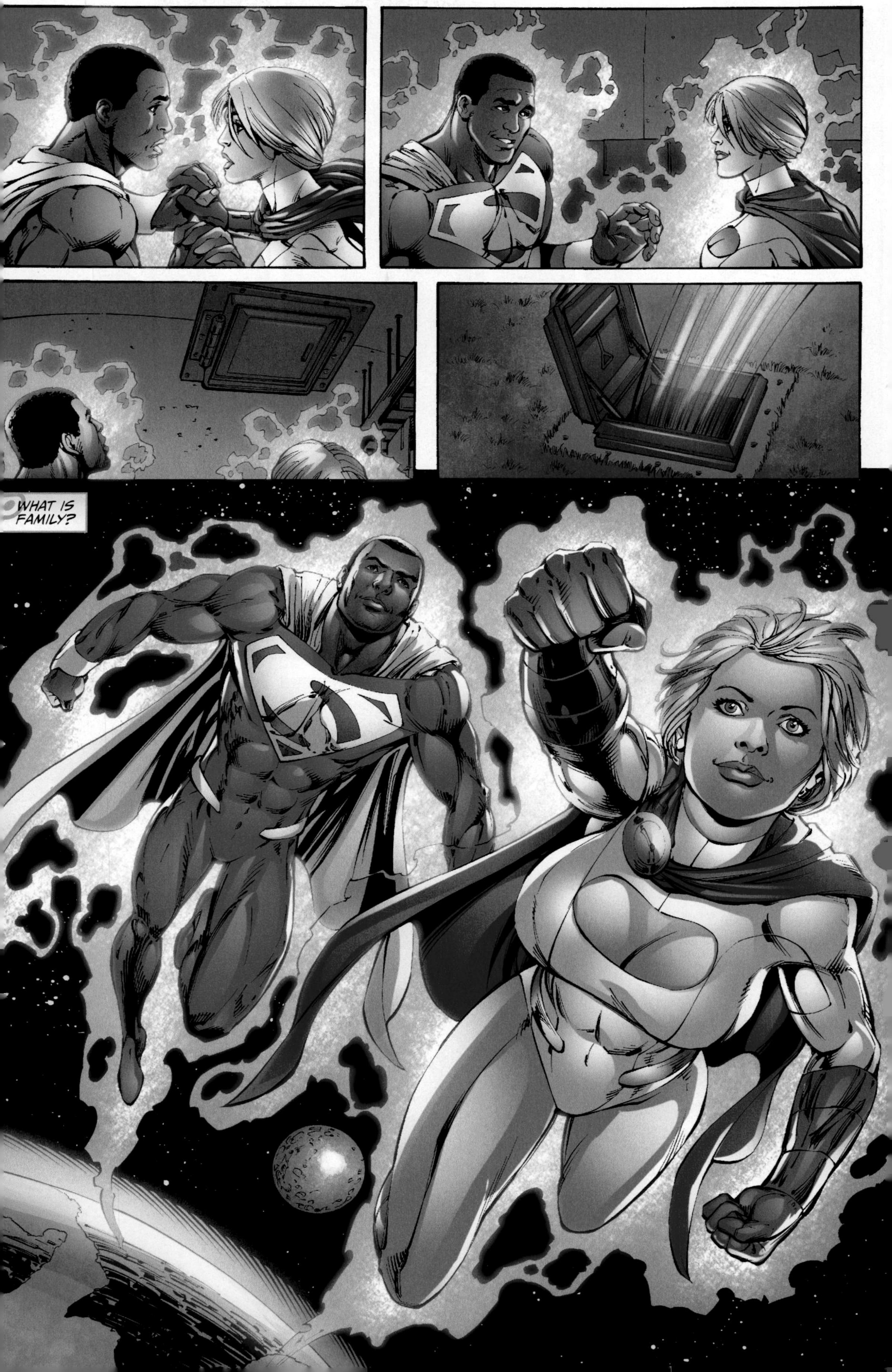
WHAT IS FAMILY?

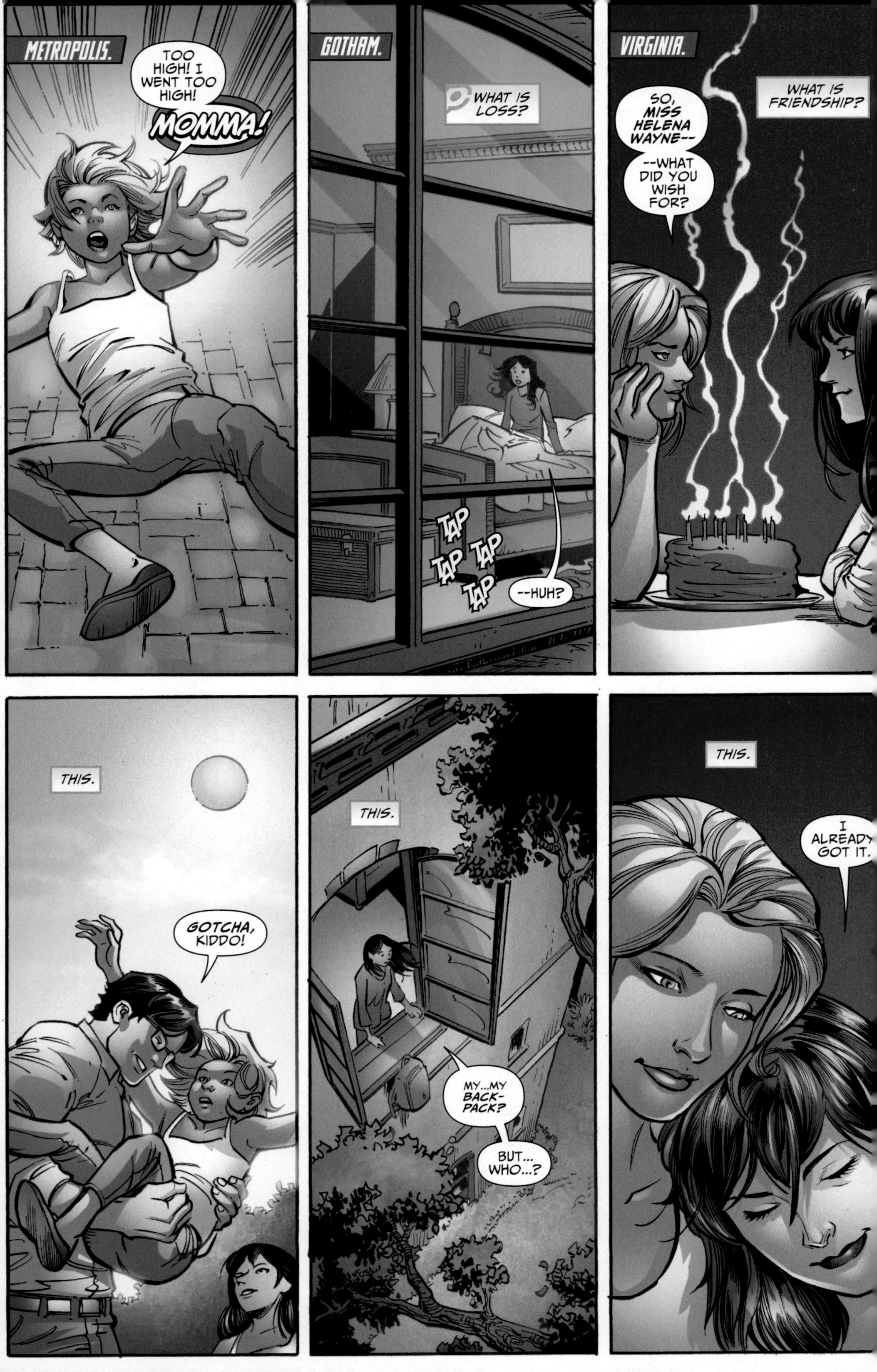
METROPOLIS.
TOO HIGH! I WENT TOO HIGH!
MOMMA!
GOTHAM.
WHAT IS LOSS?
TAP TAP TAP TAP
--HUH?
VIRGINIA.
SO, MISS HELENA WAYNE--
--WHAT DID YOU WISH FOR?
WHAT IS FRIENDSHIP?
THIS.
GOTCHA, KIDDO!
THIS.
MY...MY BACK-PACK?
BUT... WHO...?
THIS.
I ALREADY GOT IT.

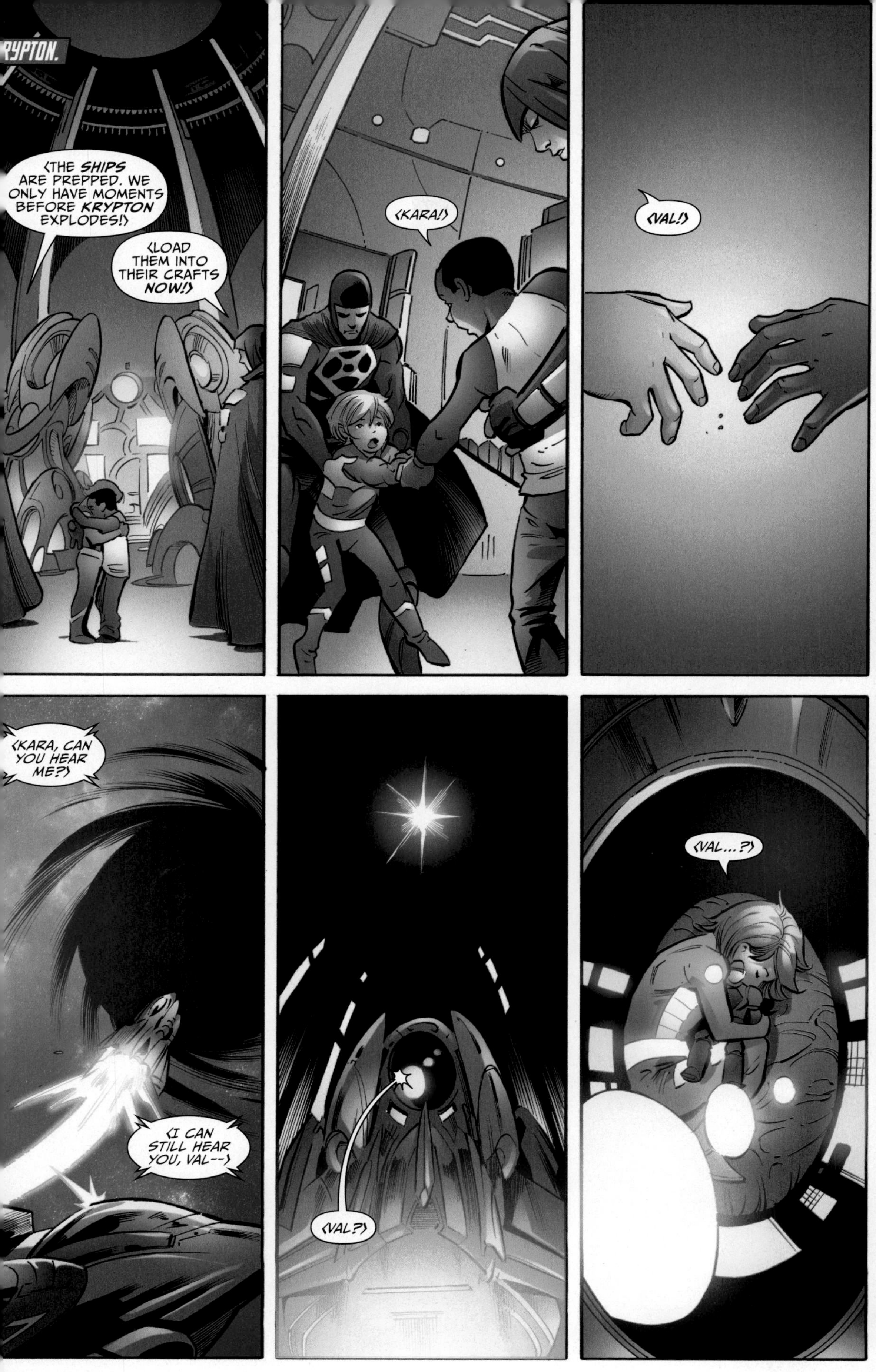

RYPTON.
<THE SHIPS ARE PREPPED. WE ONLY HAVE MOMENTS BEFORE KRYPTON EXPLODES!>
<LOAD THEM INTO THEIR CRAFTS NOW!>
<KARA!>
<VAL!>
<KARA, CAN YOU HEAR ME?>
<I CAN STILL HEAR YOU, VAL-->
<VAL?>
<VAL...?>

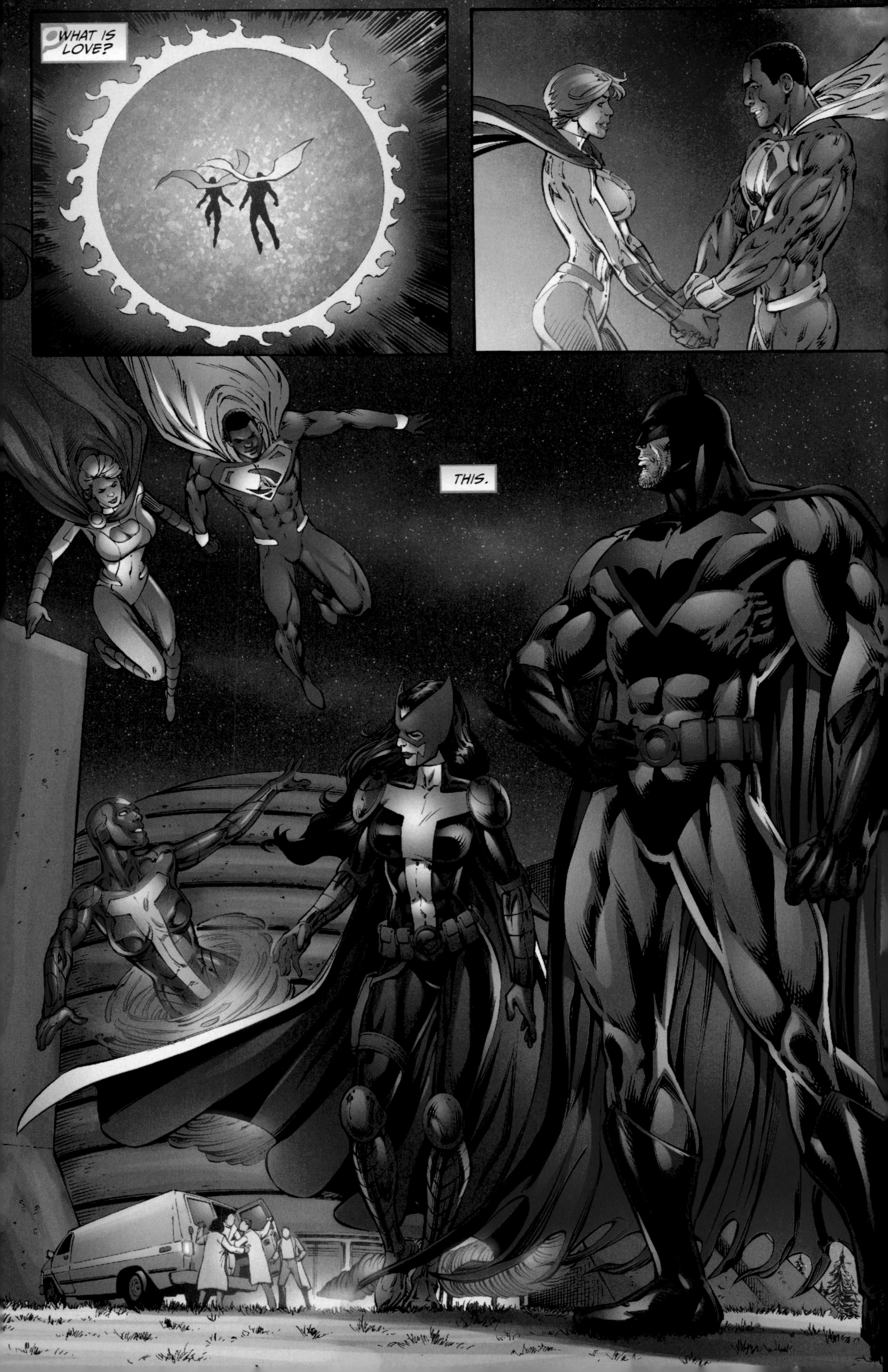
WHAT IS LOVE?
THIS.

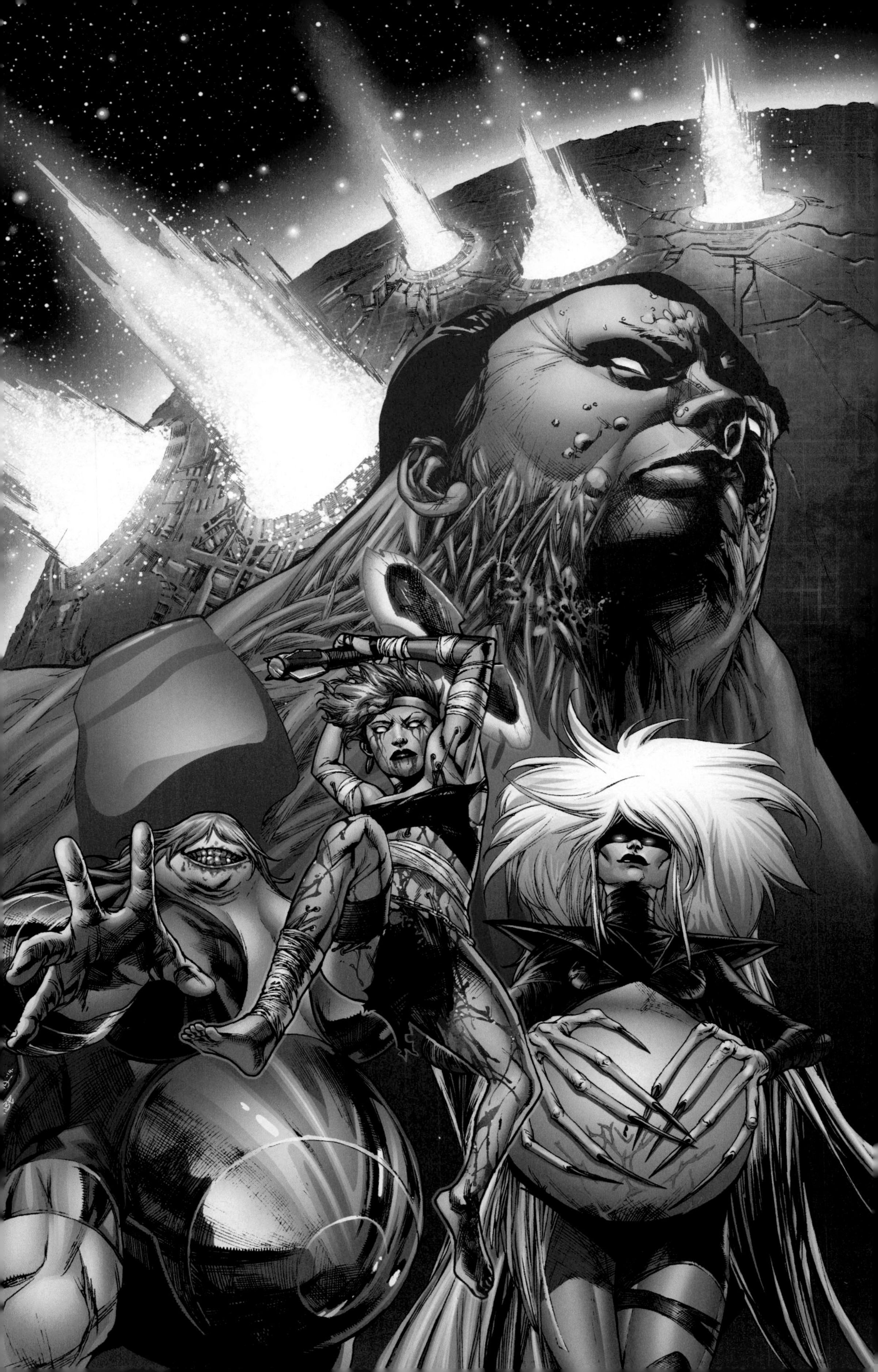

ORIGINS

TOM TAYLOR, MARGUERITE BENNETT story **MARGUERITE BENNETT** writer
ALISSON BORGES, ANDY SMITH, TREVOR SCOTT, JAVIER FERNANDEZ, DIOGENES NEVES, MARC DEERING artists
PETE PANTAZIS colorist **TAYLOR ESPOSITO** letterer cover by **STEPHEN SEGOVIA** and **GABE ELTAEB**

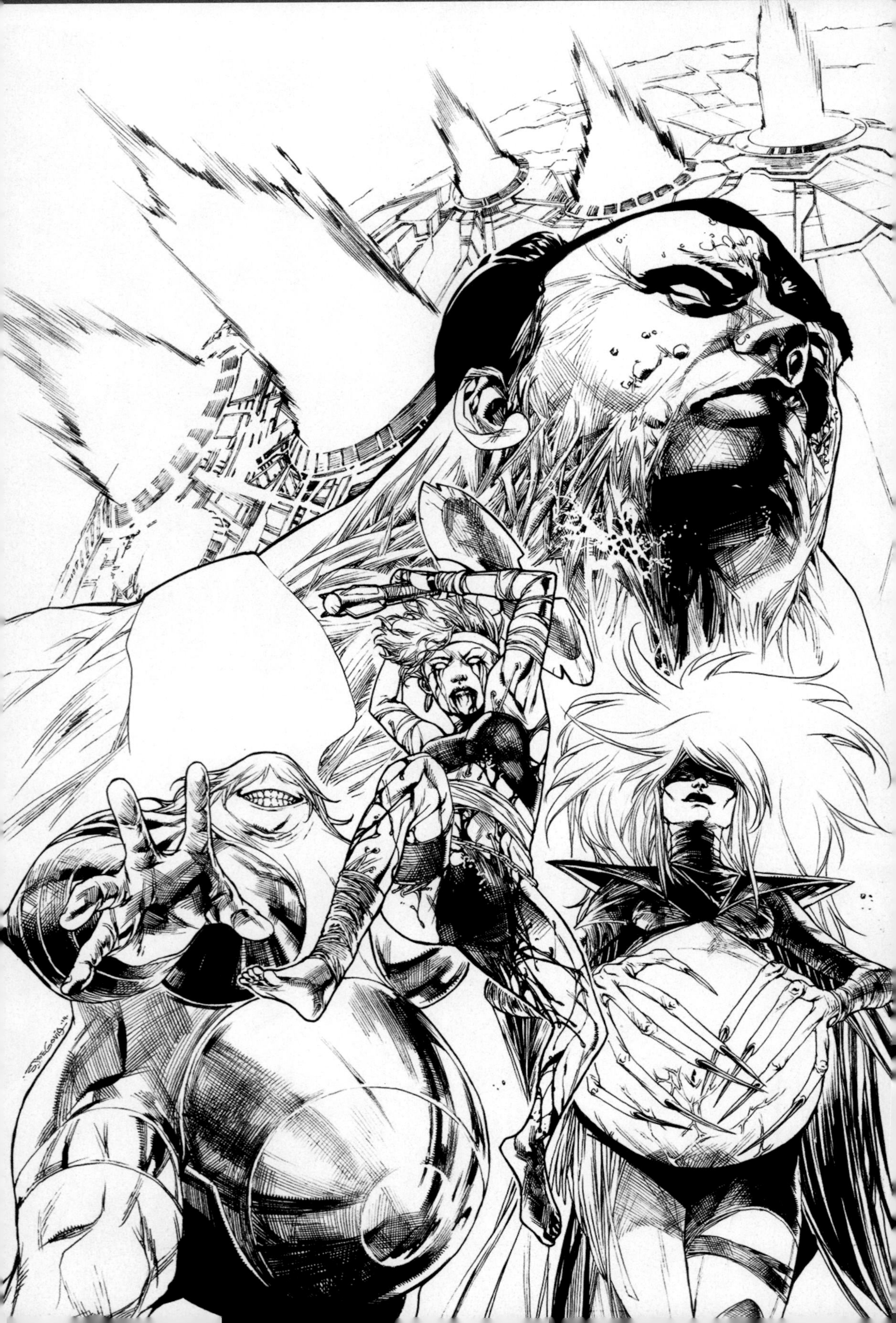

YOUR HOSPITALITY SHIRKS NOTHING, MONGUL.

EVERYTHING IN *EXCESS*, THAT'S *MY* MAXIM.

THANK YOU, DEARIE.

YOU SAW HOW *SWIFT* SHE WAS IN THE PITS, STEPPEN-WOLF? THEY NEVER IMAGINE SHE WILL BE SO SWIFT, IN HER DAZE. SHE IS LIKE A FIGHTING *DOG*, PERFECTLY TRAINED-- HAVE YOU *EVER* TRAINED SUCH A DOG?

YOU *BEAT* IT, YOU *STARVE* IT, YOU *FEED* IT CLOTTED *BLOOD*, YOU BRING IT A WOUNDED, SCREAMING THING EACH DAY WITH ITS FEED SO IT GROWS TO LOVE THE *SOUNDS* OF *SCREAMS*--

OH, YOU'RE MAKING MY PETS NERVOUS, *LORD MONGUL*.

MY PACK.

ALL THAT IS *BEHIND* ME, SWEETS, NEVER FEAR. I AM LEADER OF THE PACK NOW--

YOUR PACK, LORD MONGUL.

YOU HAVE SEEN THE MIGHT OF OUR WORLD, STEPPEN-WOLF. WHAT MORE CAN YOU ASK?

WHAT DO YOU KNOW OF *DEATH*, MONGUL?

DEATH? THE ARENAS ARE CHARNEL PITS. DEATH IS A *PETTY* THING, COMMON AS BREATH. DEATH IS *NOTHING*.

AND YOU?

DEATH... DEATH IS...

...*EVERYTHING*.

..AND
BITE!

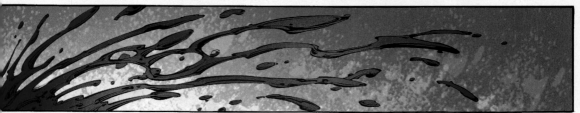

YOU
BRED A *MAD*
DOG. WHAT DID
YOU *THINK* IT
WOULD DO?

YOUR
MAD DOG NOW.
TAKE CARE, FOR
YOU HAVE LEARNED
HOW *FAITHFUL*
SHE IS...

HOW
AMBITIOUS...

YOUR
FURY OF
FAMINE...

...SO
HUNGRY FOR
LIFE.

THE BEGINNING...

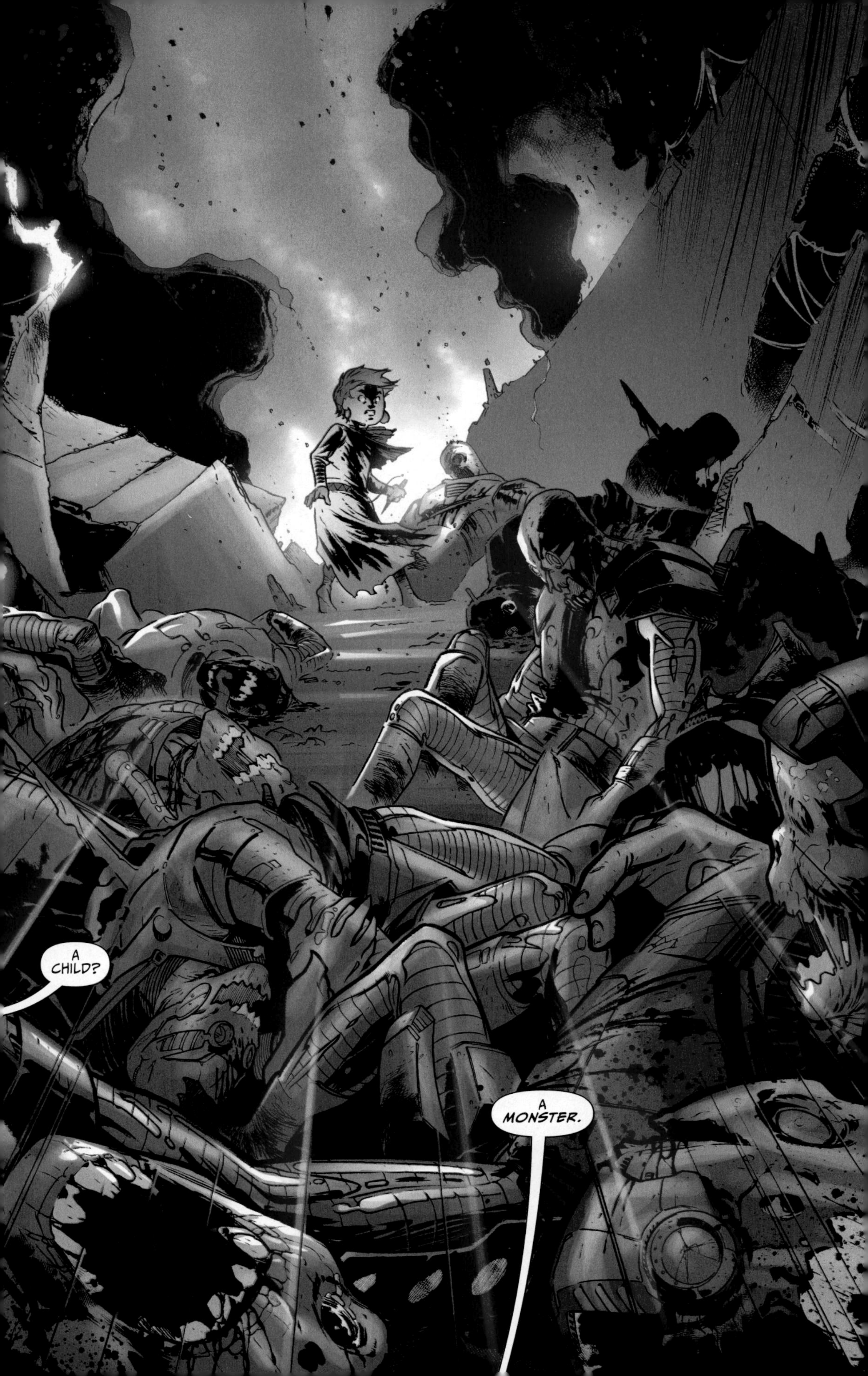
A CHILD?
A MONSTER.

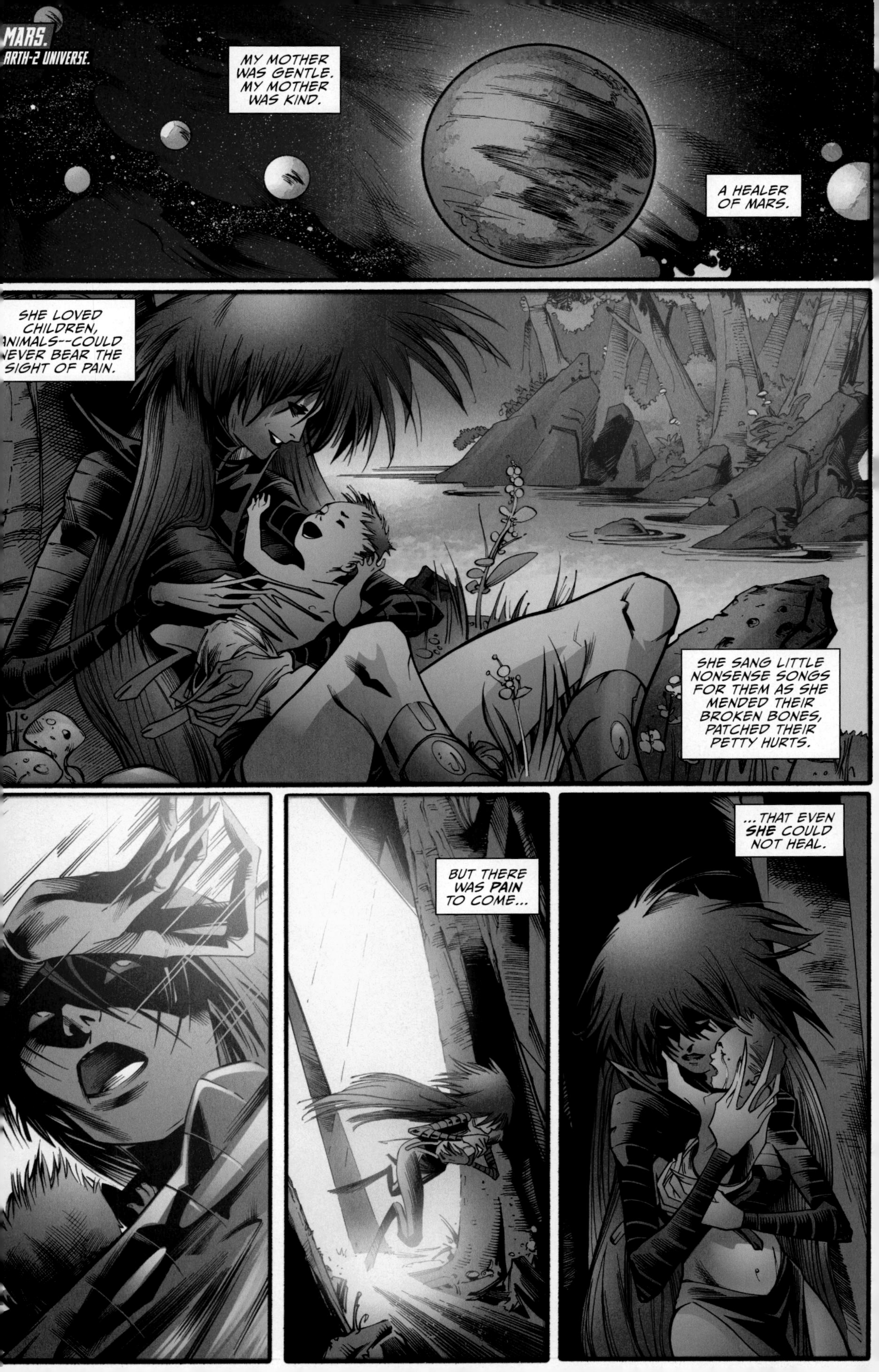
MARS.
ARTH-2 UNIVERSE.
MY MOTHER WAS GENTLE. MY MOTHER WAS KIND.
A HEALER OF MARS.
SHE LOVED CHILDREN, ANIMALS--COULD NEVER BEAR THE SIGHT OF PAIN.
SHE SANG LITTLE NONSENSE SONGS FOR THEM AS SHE MENDED THEIR BROKEN BONES, PATCHED THEIR PETTY HURTS.
BUT THERE WAS PAIN TO COME...
...THAT EVEN SHE COULD NOT HEAL.

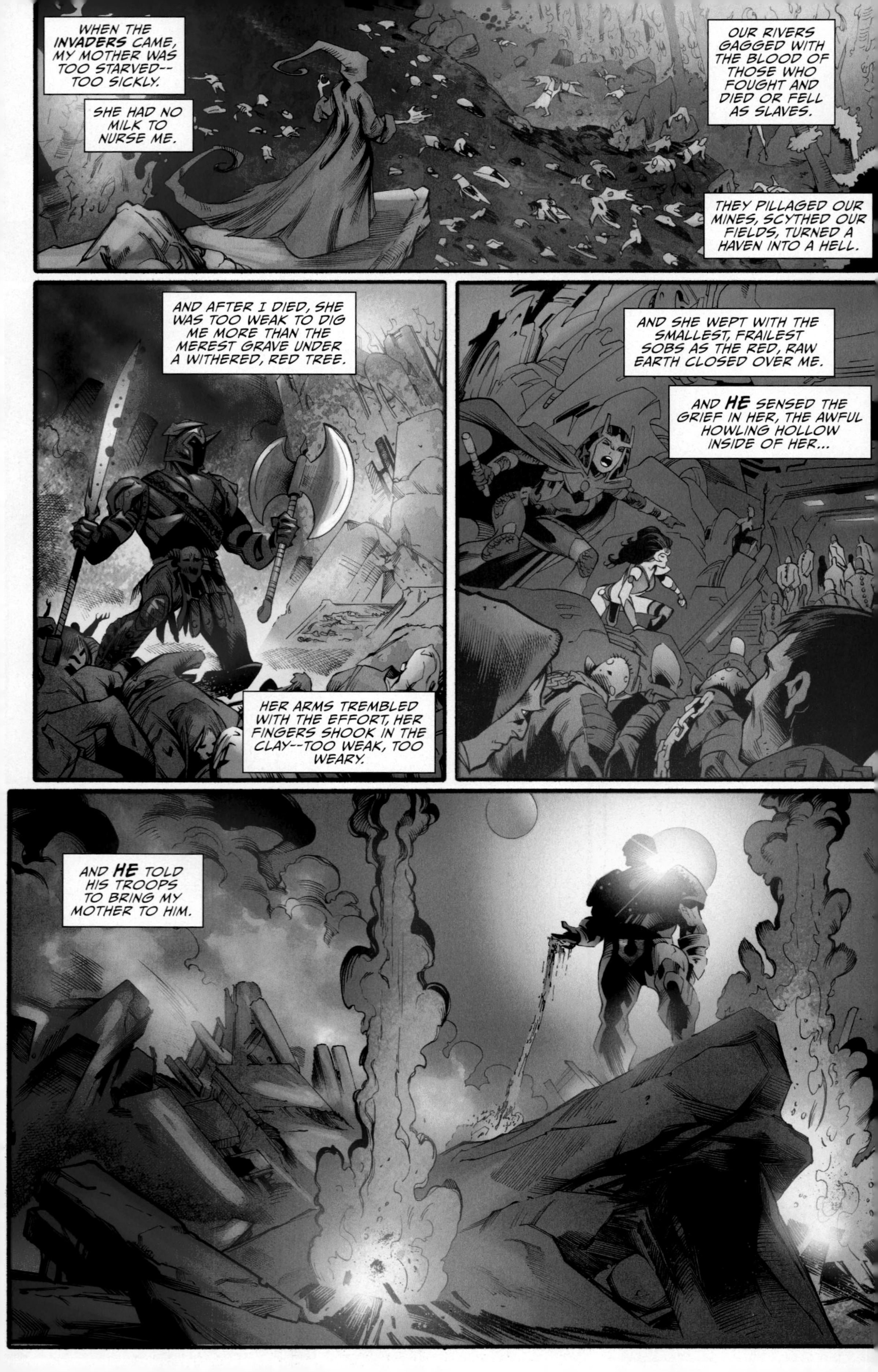
WHEN THE INVADERS CAME, MY MOTHER WAS TOO STARVED-- TOO SICKLY.
SHE HAD NO MILK TO NURSE ME.
OUR RIVERS GAGGED WITH THE BLOOD OF THOSE WHO FOUGHT AND DIED OR FELL AS SLAVES.
THEY PILLAGED OUR MINES, SCYTHED OUR FIELDS, TURNED A HAVEN INTO A HELL.
AND AFTER I DIED, SHE WAS TOO WEAK TO DIG ME MORE THAN THE MEREST GRAVE UNDER A WITHERED, RED TREE.
HER ARMS TREMBLED WITH THE EFFORT, HER FINGERS SHOOK IN THE CLAY--TOO WEAK, TOO WEARY.
AND SHE WEPT WITH THE SMALLEST, FRAILEST SOBS AS THE RED, RAW EARTH CLOSED OVER ME.
AND HE SENSED THE GRIEF IN HER, THE AWFUL HOWLING HOLLOW INSIDE OF HER...
AND HE TOLD HIS TROOPS TO BRING MY MOTHER TO HIM.

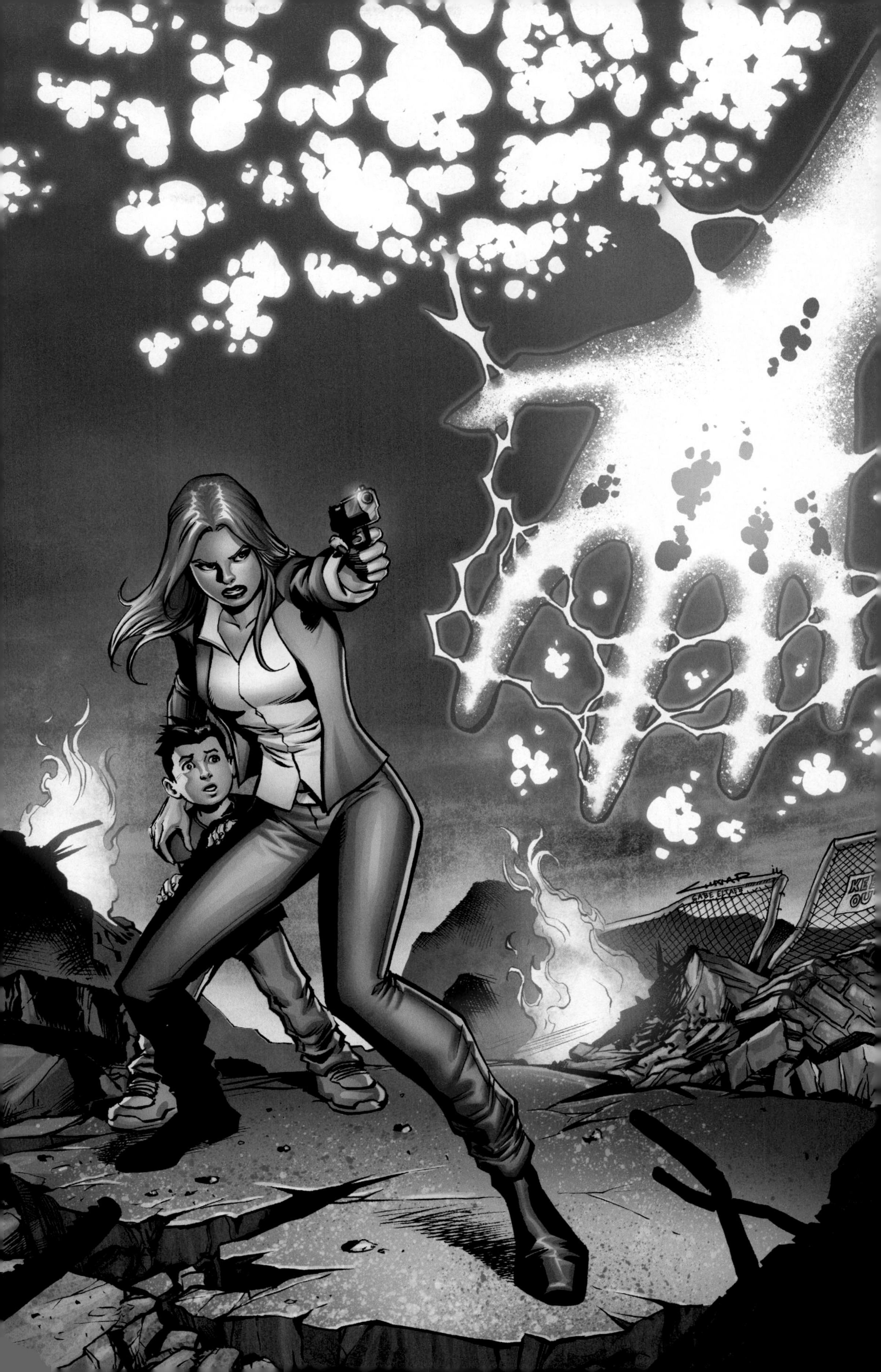

FLAGITIOUS

MARGUERITE BENNETT, MIKE JOHNSON writers ANDY SMITH penciller TREVOR SCOTT inker
PETER PANTAZIS, MATT YACKEY, ANDREW DALHOUSE colorists CARLOS M. MANGUAL letterer cover by YILDIRAY CINAR and GABE ELTAEB

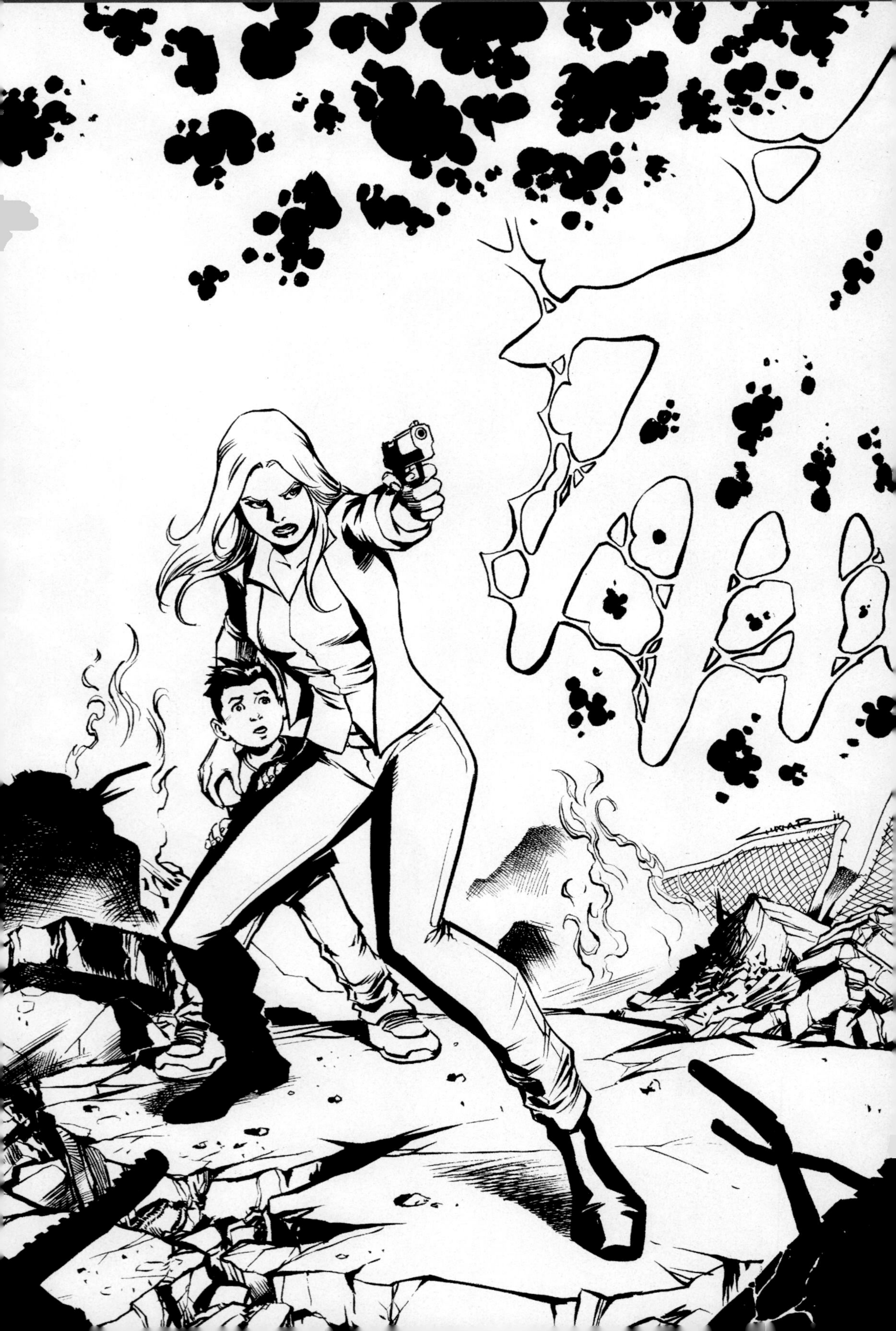

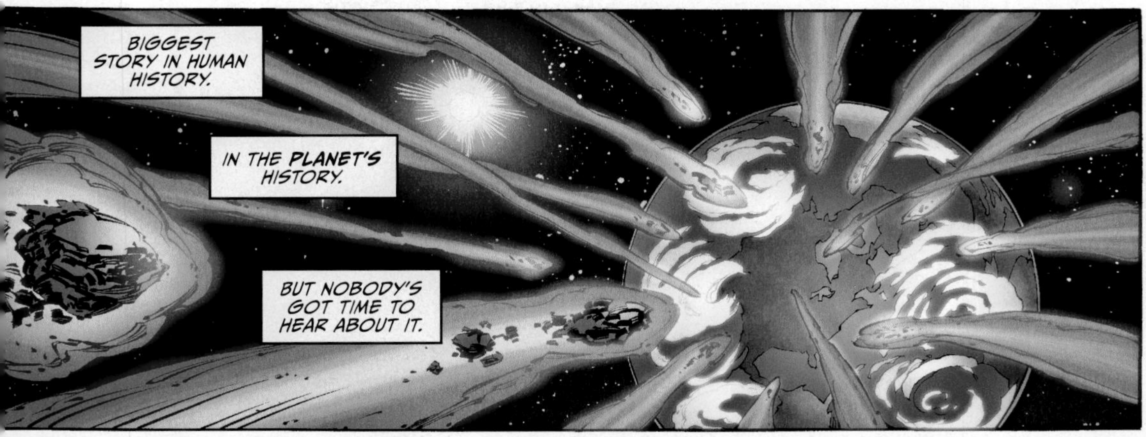
BIGGEST STORY IN HUMAN HISTORY.
IN THE **PLANET'S** HISTORY.
BUT NOBODY'S GOT TIME TO HEAR ABOUT IT.

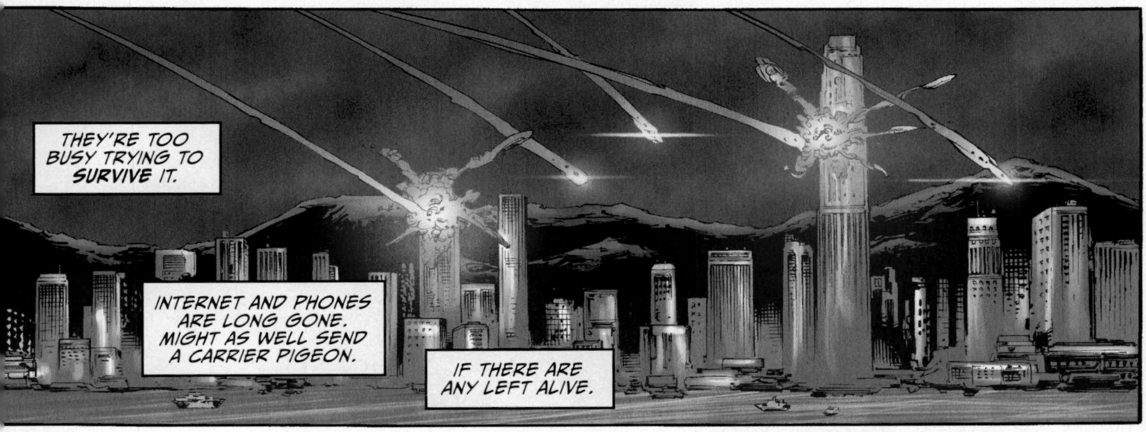
THEY'RE TOO BUSY TRYING TO **SURVIVE** IT.
INTERNET AND PHONES ARE LONG GONE. MIGHT AS WELL SEND A CARRIER PIGEON.
IF THERE ARE ANY LEFT ALIVE.

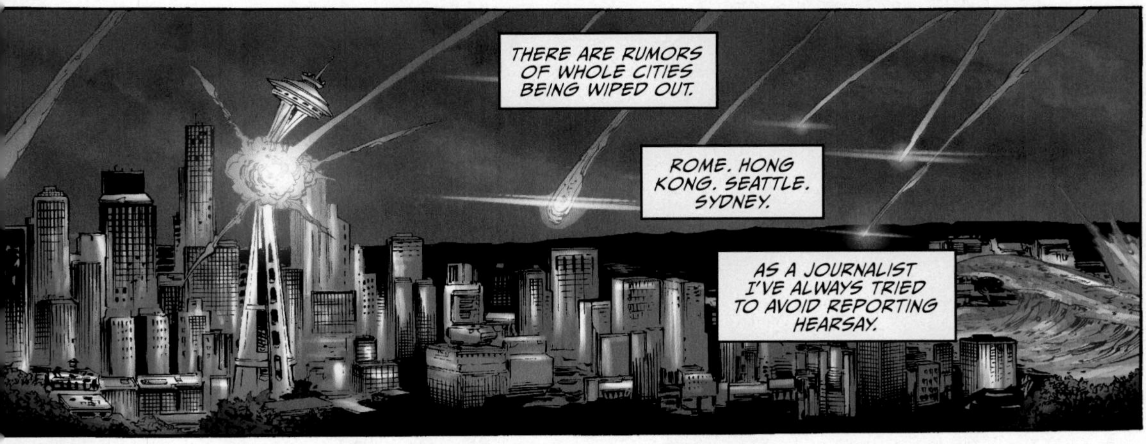
THERE ARE RUMORS OF WHOLE CITIES BEING WIPED OUT.
ROME. HONG KONG. SEATTLE. SYDNEY.
AS A JOURNALIST I'VE ALWAYS TRIED TO AVOID REPORTING HEARSAY.

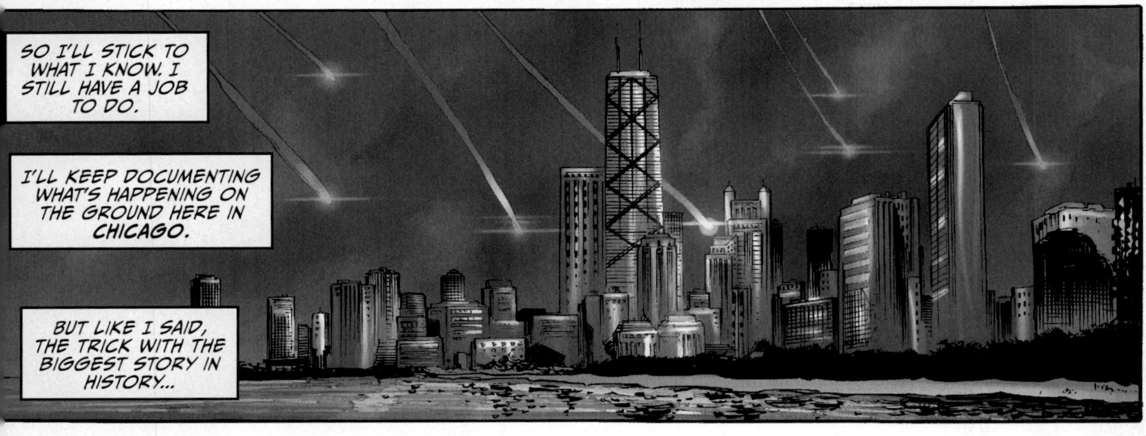
SO I'LL STICK TO WHAT I KNOW. I STILL HAVE A JOB TO DO.
I'LL KEEP DOCUMENTING WHAT'S HAPPENING ON THE GROUND HERE IN **CHICAGO**.
BUT LIKE I SAID, THE TRICK WITH THE BIGGEST STORY IN HISTORY...

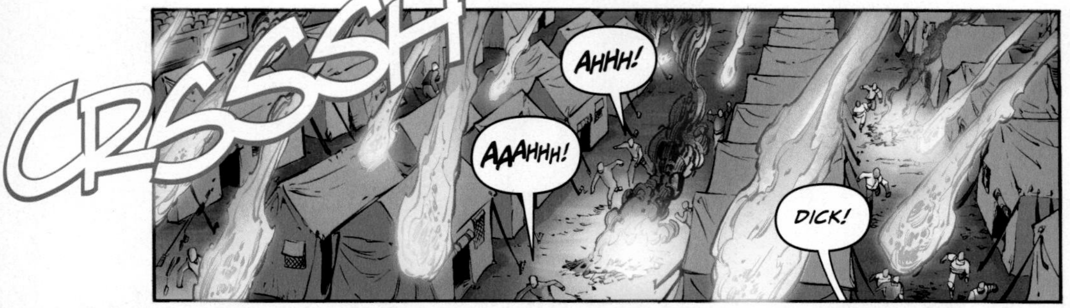
CRSSSH
AHHH!
AAAHHH!
DICK!

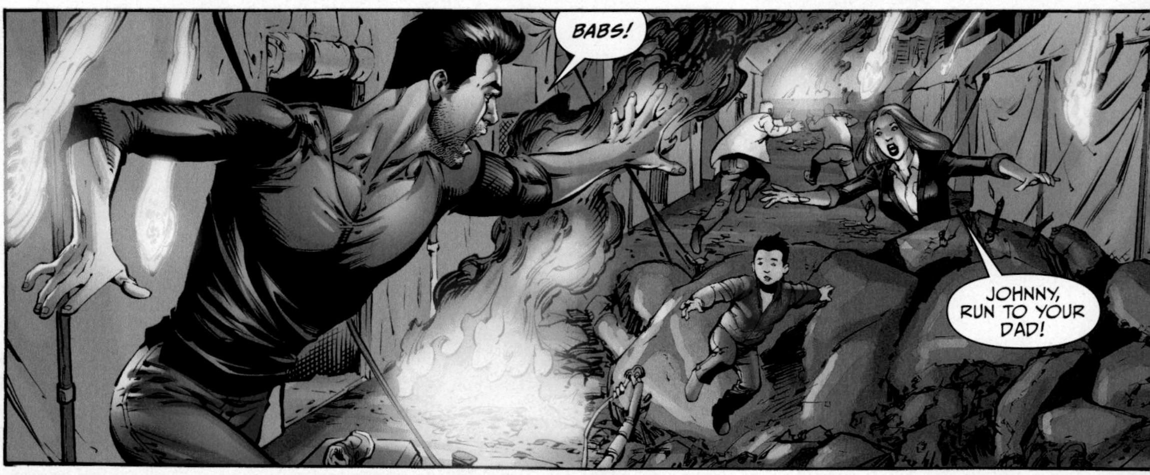
BABS!
JOHNNY, RUN TO YOUR DAD!

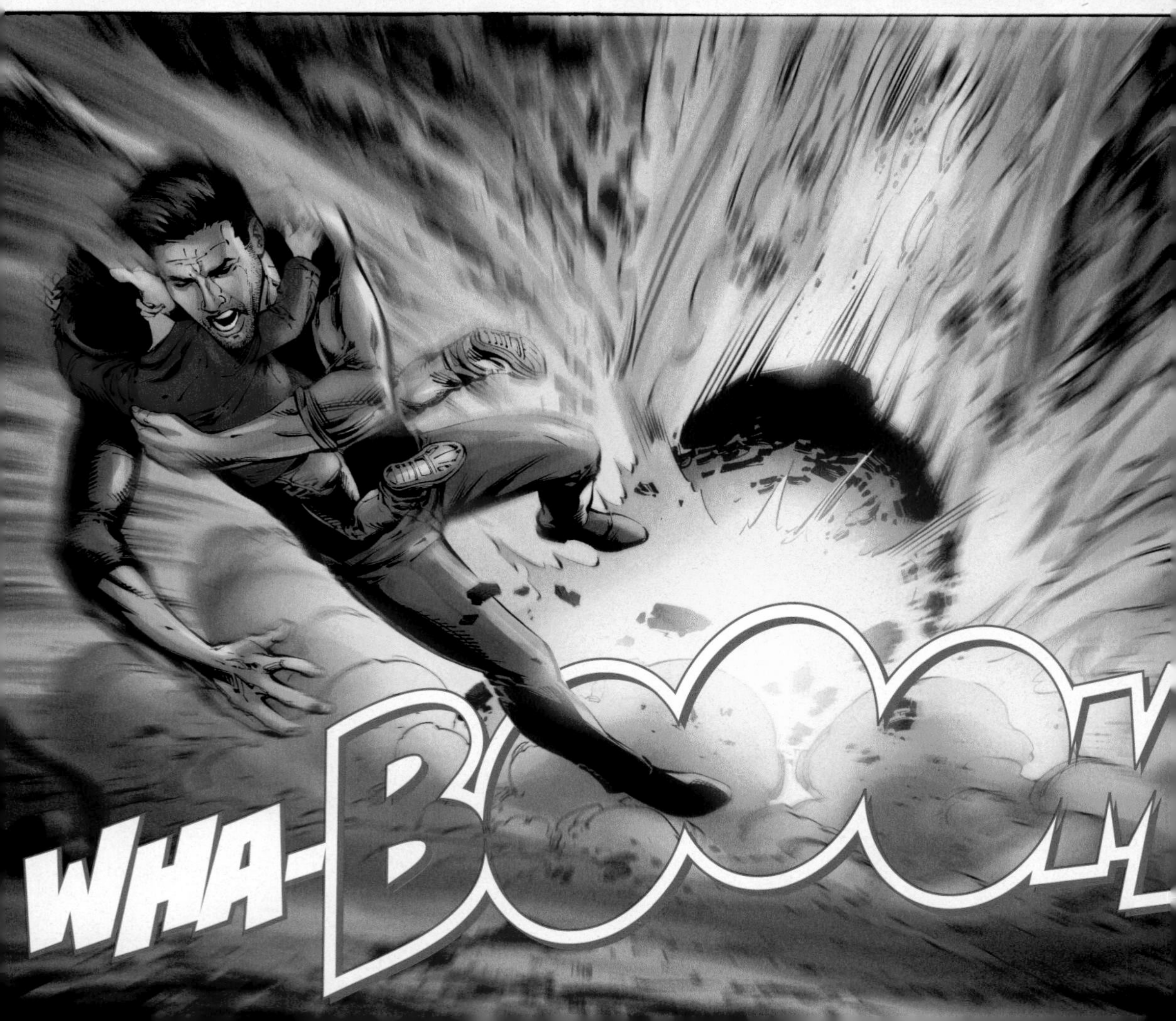
WHA-BOOOM

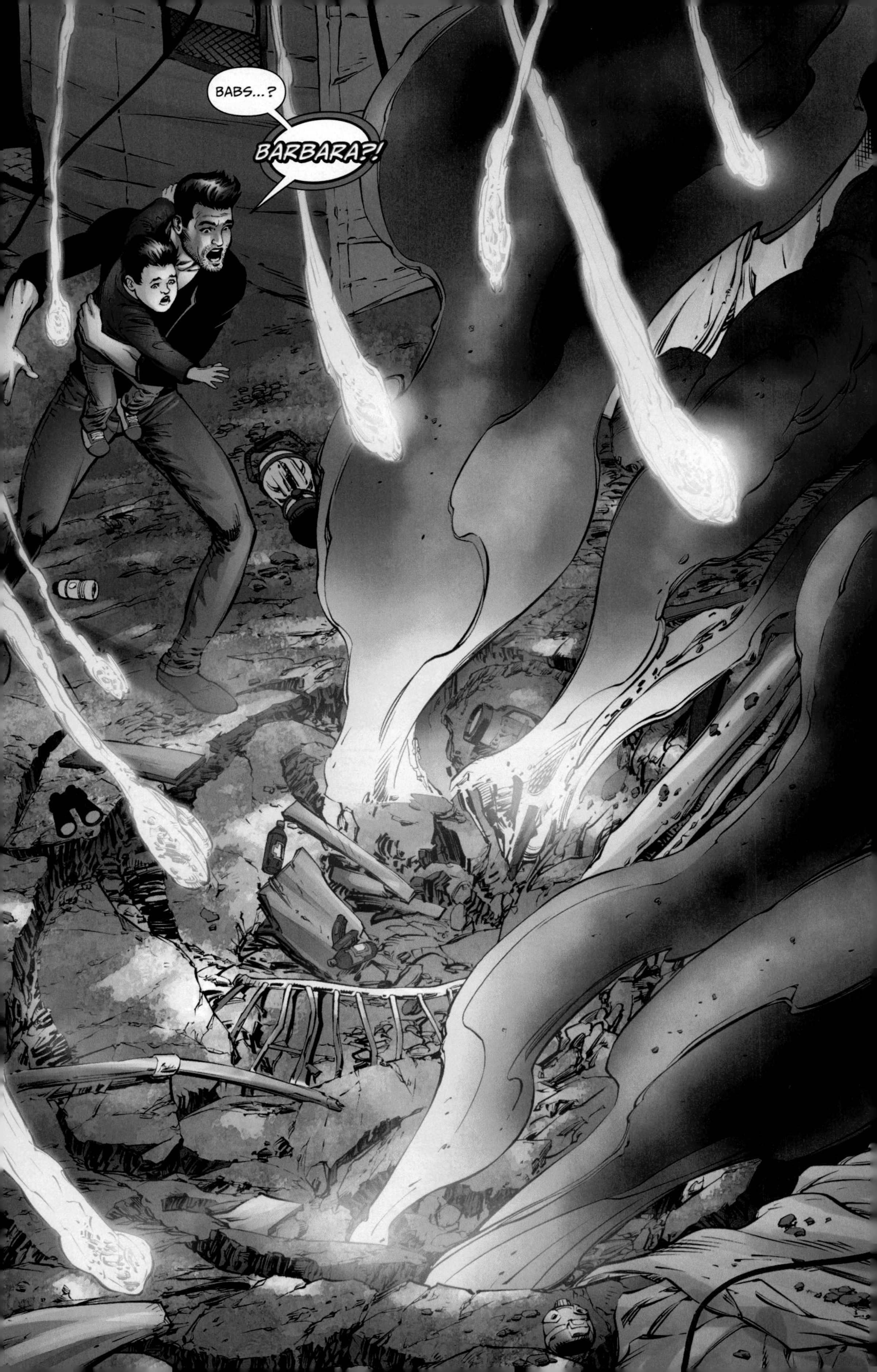
BABS...?
BARBARA?!

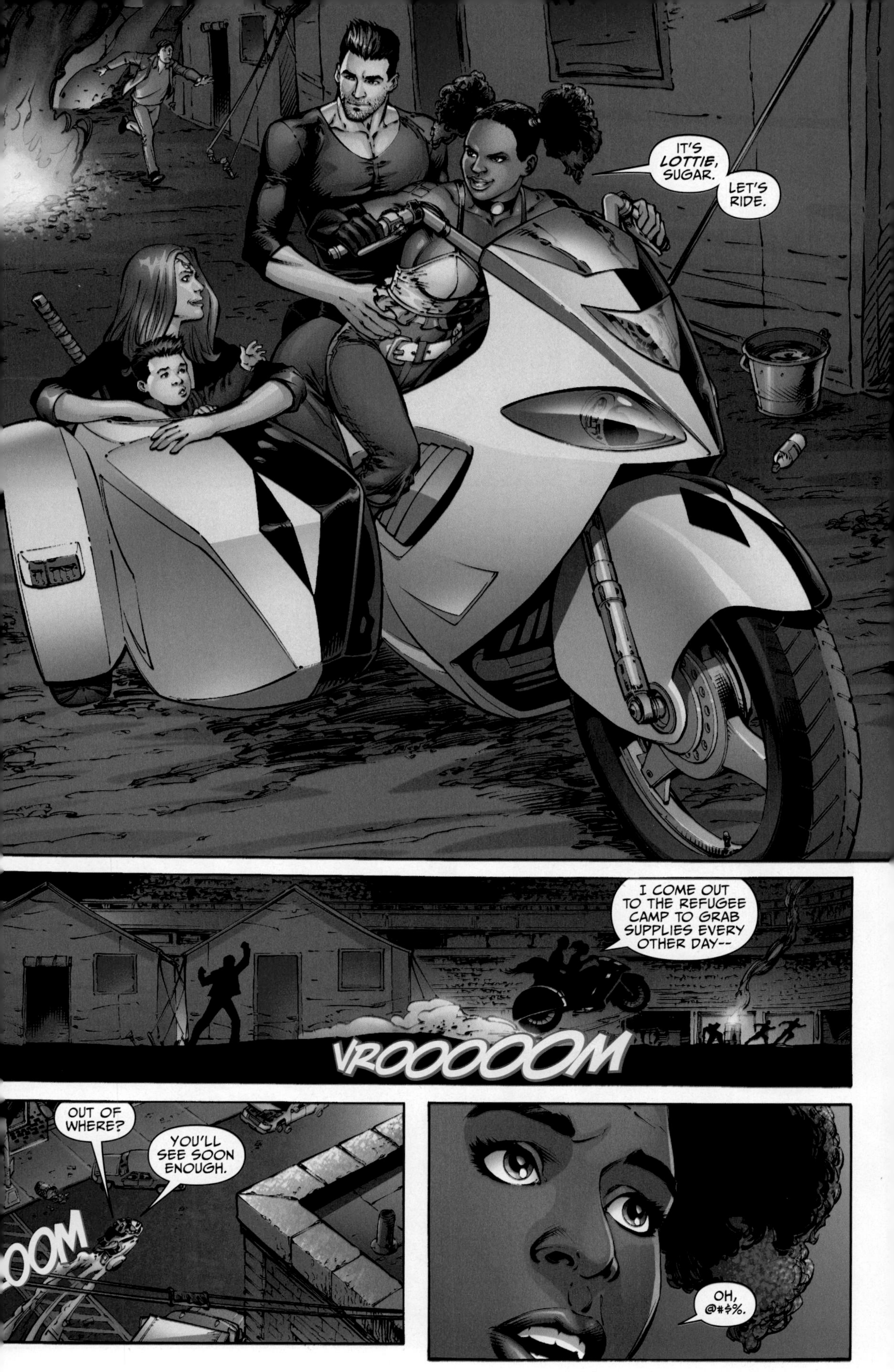
IT'S LOTTIE, SUGAR.
LET'S RIDE.
I COME OUT TO THE REFUGEE CAMP TO GRAB SUPPLIES EVERY OTHER DAY--
VROOOOOM
OUT OF WHERE?
YOU'LL SEE SOON ENOUGH.
OOM
OH, @#$%.

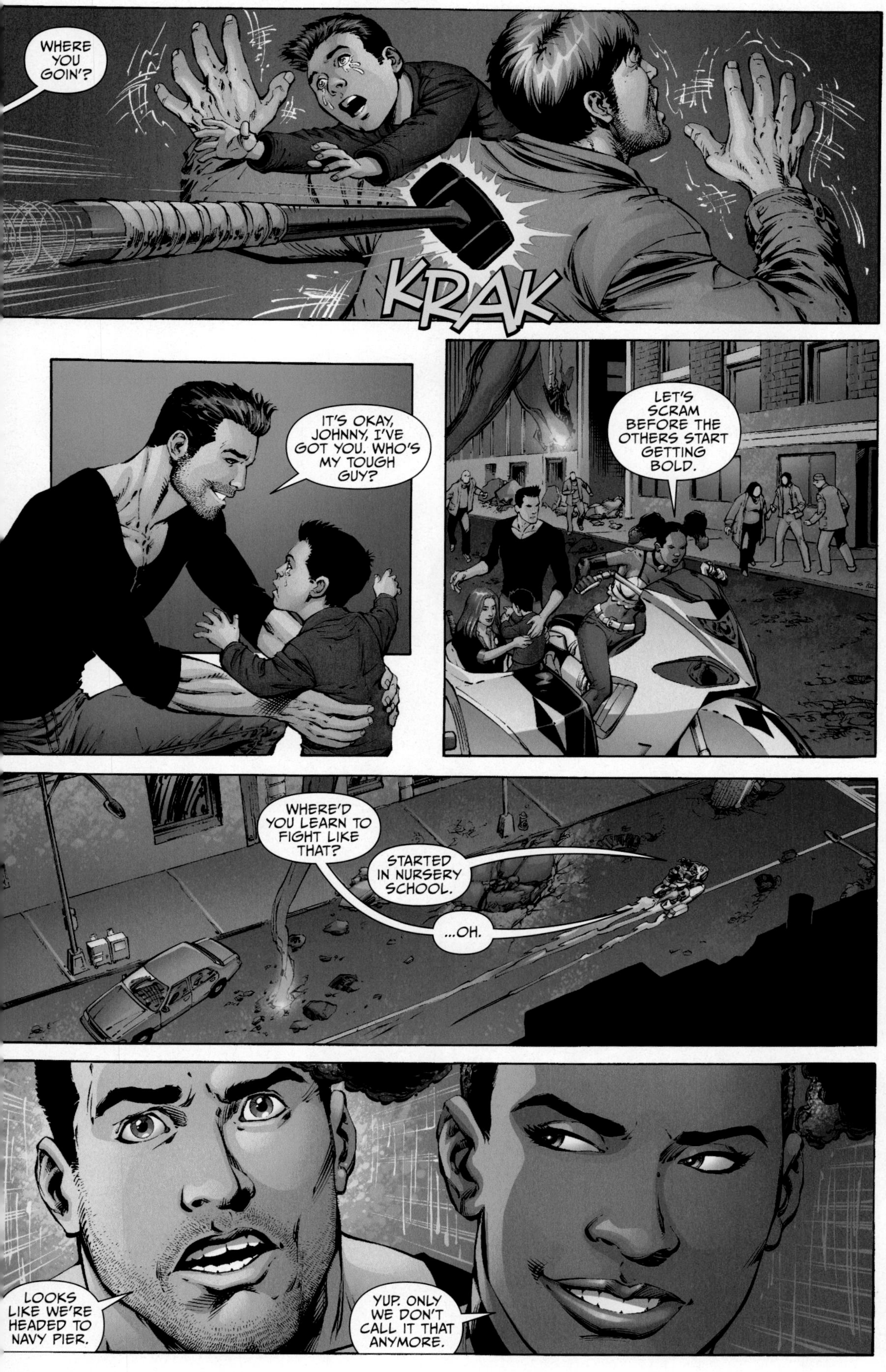
WHERE YOU GOIN'?
KRAK
IT'S OKAY, JOHNNY, I'VE GOT YOU. WHO'S MY TOUGH GUY?
LET'S SCRAM BEFORE THE OTHERS START GETTING BOLD.
WHERE'D YOU LEARN TO FIGHT LIKE THAT?
STARTED IN NURSERY SCHOOL.
...OH.
LOOKS LIKE WE'RE HEADED TO NAVY PIER.
YUP. ONLY WE DON'T CALL IT THAT ANYMORE.

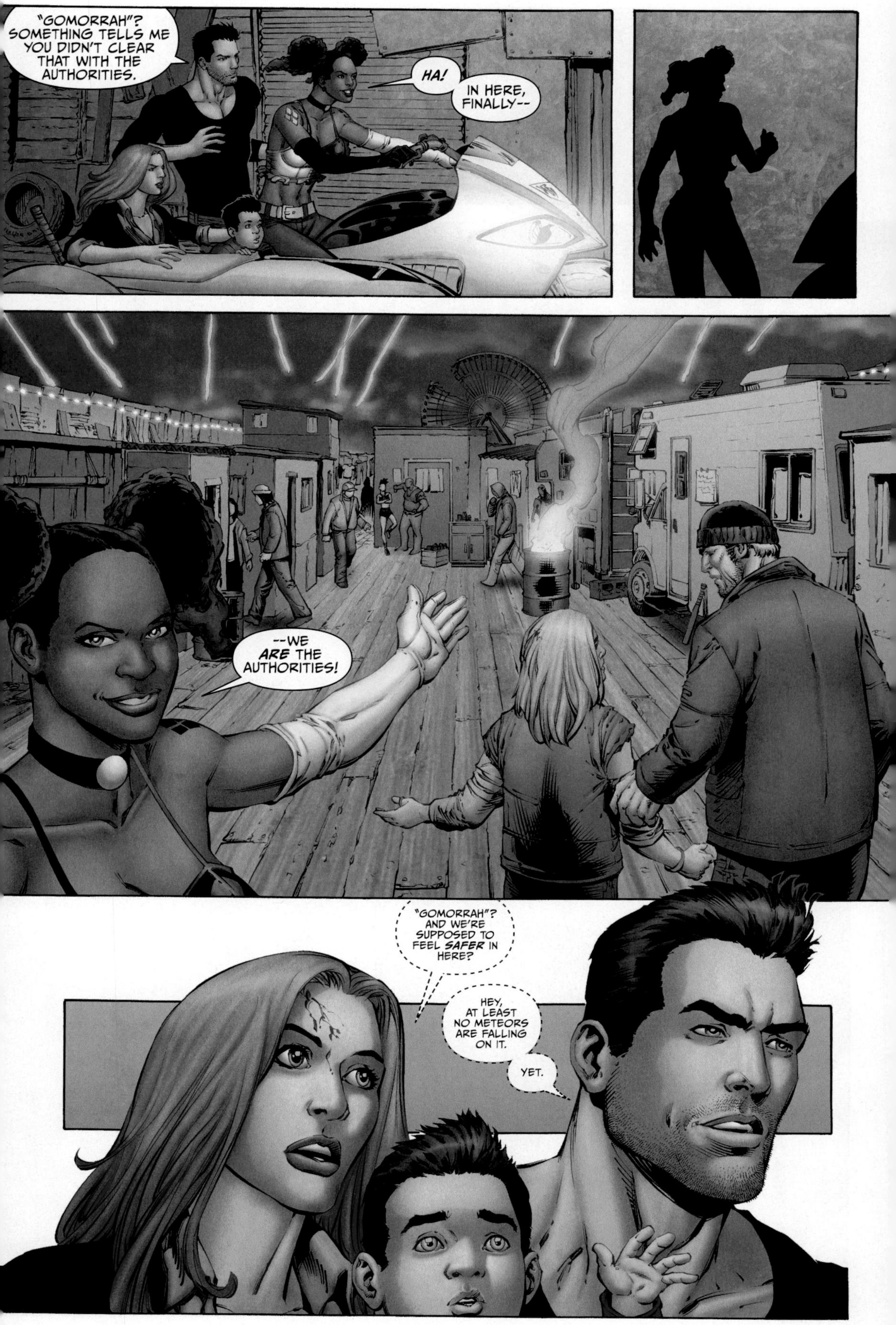
"GOMORRAH"? SOMETHING TELLS ME YOU DIDN'T CLEAR THAT WITH THE AUTHORITIES.
HA!
IN HERE, FINALLY--
--WE ARE THE AUTHORITIES!
"GOMORRAH"? AND WE'RE SUPPOSED TO FEEL SAFER IN HERE?
HEY, AT LEAST NO METEORS ARE FALLING ON IT.
YET.

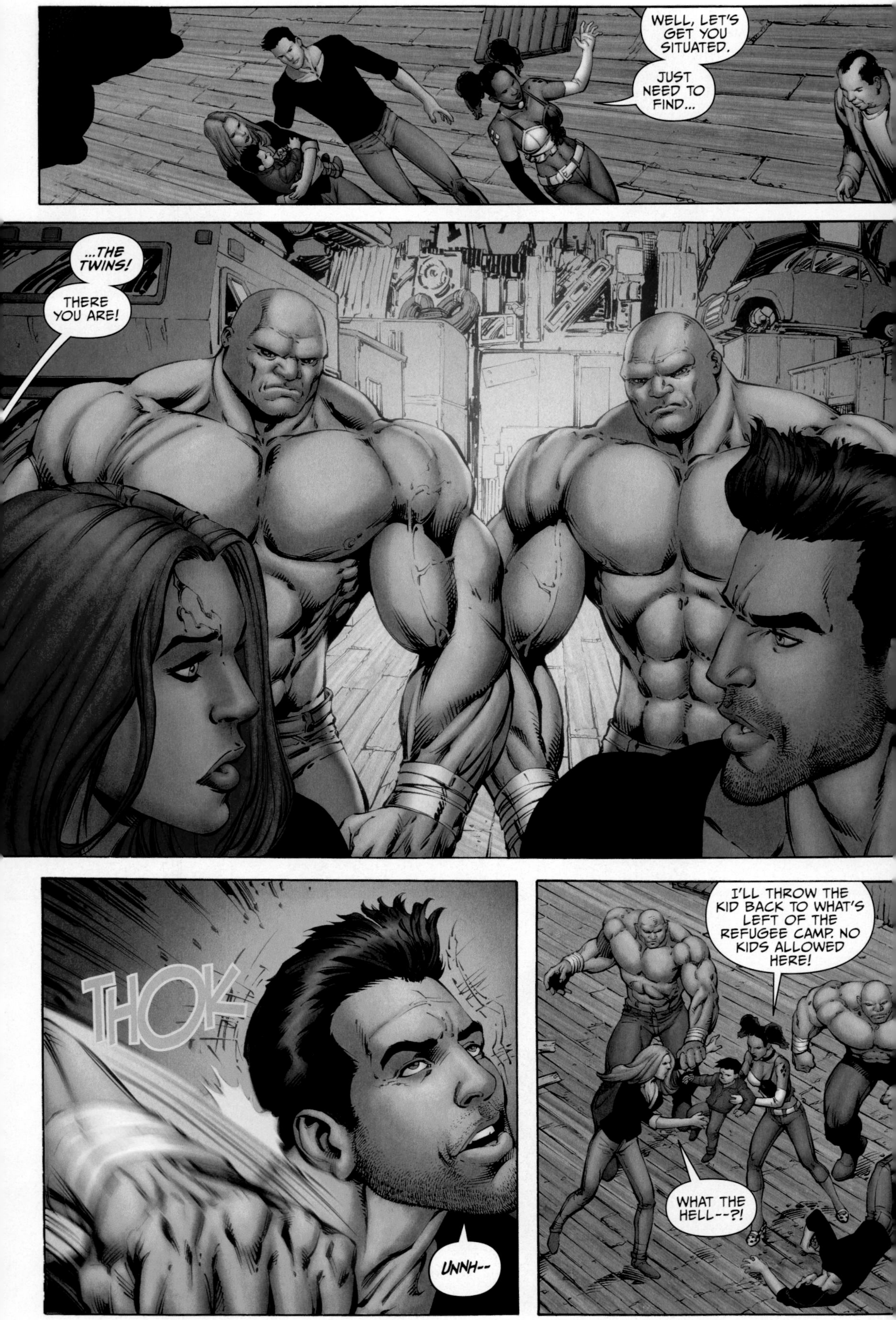
WELL, LET'S GET YOU SITUATED.
JUST NEED TO FIND...
...THE TWINS!
THERE YOU ARE!
THOK
UNNH--
I'LL THROW THE KID BACK TO WHAT'S LEFT OF THE REFUGEE CAMP. NO KIDS ALLOWED HERE!
WHAT THE HELL--?!

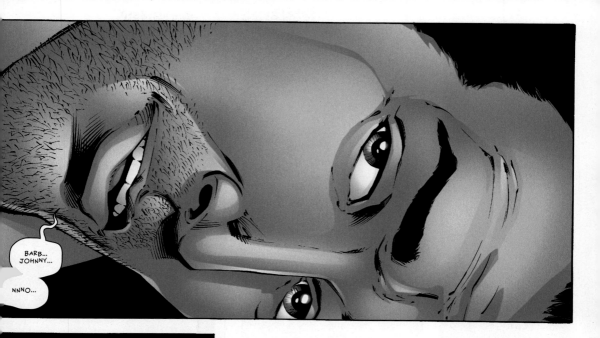

BARB... JOHNNY...

NNNO...

DON'T WORRY, "BARB."

WE JUST LOVE COPS HERE!

HEY, DICK, DON'T WORRY...

THE FUN'S JUST GETTING STARTED!

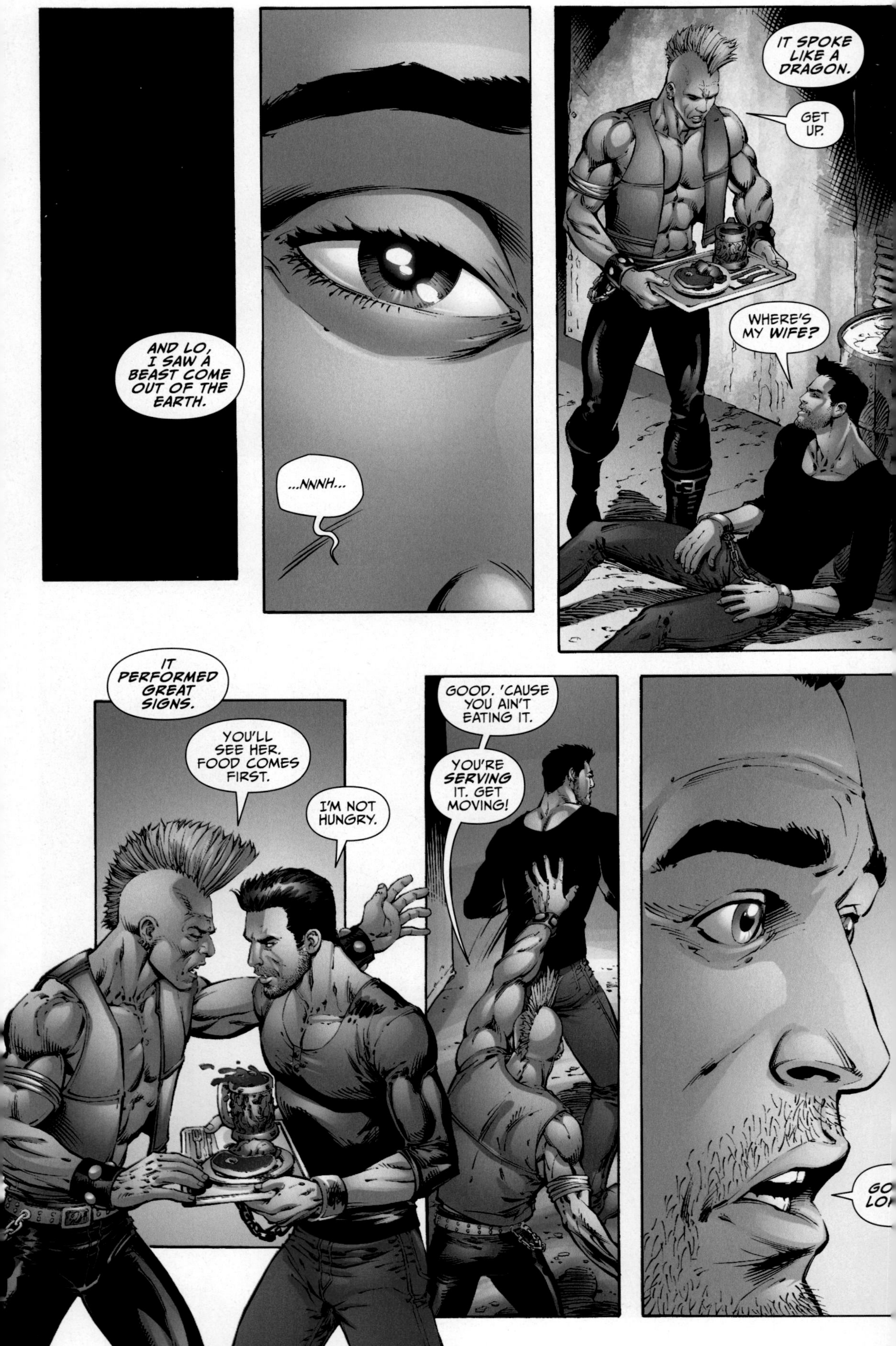
AND LO, I SAW A BEAST COME OUT OF THE EARTH.
...NNNH...
IT SPOKE LIKE A DRAGON.
GET UP.
WHERE'S MY WIFE?
IT PERFORMED GREAT SIGNS.
YOU'LL SEE HER. FOOD COMES FIRST.
I'M NOT HUNGRY.
GOOD. 'CAUSE YOU AIN'T EATING IT.
YOU'RE SERVING IT. GET MOVING!

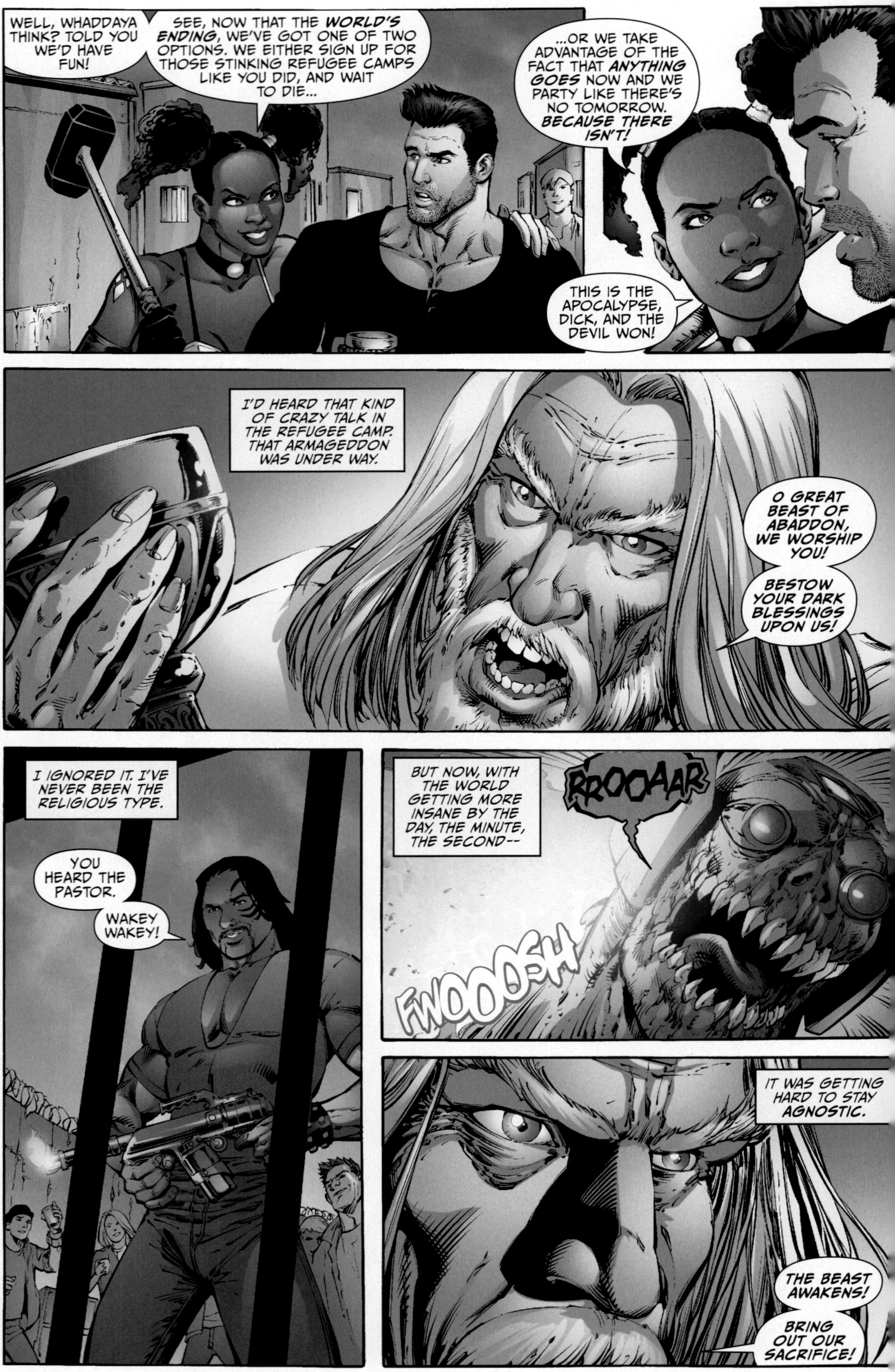

WELL, WHADDAYA THINK? TOLD YOU WE'D HAVE FUN!
SEE, NOW THAT THE WORLD'S ENDING, WE'VE GOT ONE OF TWO OPTIONS. WE EITHER SIGN UP FOR THOSE STINKING REFUGEE CAMPS LIKE YOU DID, AND WAIT TO DIE...
...OR WE TAKE ADVANTAGE OF THE FACT THAT ANYTHING GOES NOW AND WE PARTY LIKE THERE'S NO TOMORROW. BECAUSE THERE ISN'T!
THIS IS THE APOCALYPSE, DICK, AND THE DEVIL WON!
I'D HEARD THAT KIND OF CRAZY TALK IN THE REFUGEE CAMP. THAT ARMAGEDDON WAS UNDER WAY.
O GREAT BEAST OF ABADDON, WE WORSHIP YOU!
BESTOW YOUR DARK BLESSINGS UPON US!
I IGNORED IT. I'VE NEVER BEEN THE RELIGIOUS TYPE.
YOU HEARD THE PASTOR.
WAKEY WAKEY!
BUT NOW, WITH THE WORLD GETTING MORE INSANE BY THE DAY, THE MINUTE, THE SECOND--
RROOAAR
FWOOOSH
IT WAS GETTING HARD TO STAY AGNOSTIC.
THE BEAST AWAKENS!
BRING OUT OUR SACRIFICE!

JUST SO WE'RE CLEAR--

--I WAS TOTALLY ABOUT TO ESCAPE BEFORE YOU RESCUED ME.

WRROOOM

NO DOUBT.

I HAVE TO ADMIT, THOUGH, IT WAS KIND OF *SEXY* SEEING MY HUSBAND IN ACTION.

YEAH, WELL, LET'S HOPE IT'S THE LAST TIME.

LET'S JUST GET BACK TO JOHNNY AND HOPE THOSE *REFUGEE TRAINS* ARE FINALLY ROLLING OUT OF THE CITY.

WE'LL FIND A NEW HOME. A SAFE PLACE TO START OVER.

I HEAR MYSEL SAY TH WORD

EVERYTHING'S GOING TO BE ALL RIGHT.

I JUST WISH I BELIEVED THEM.

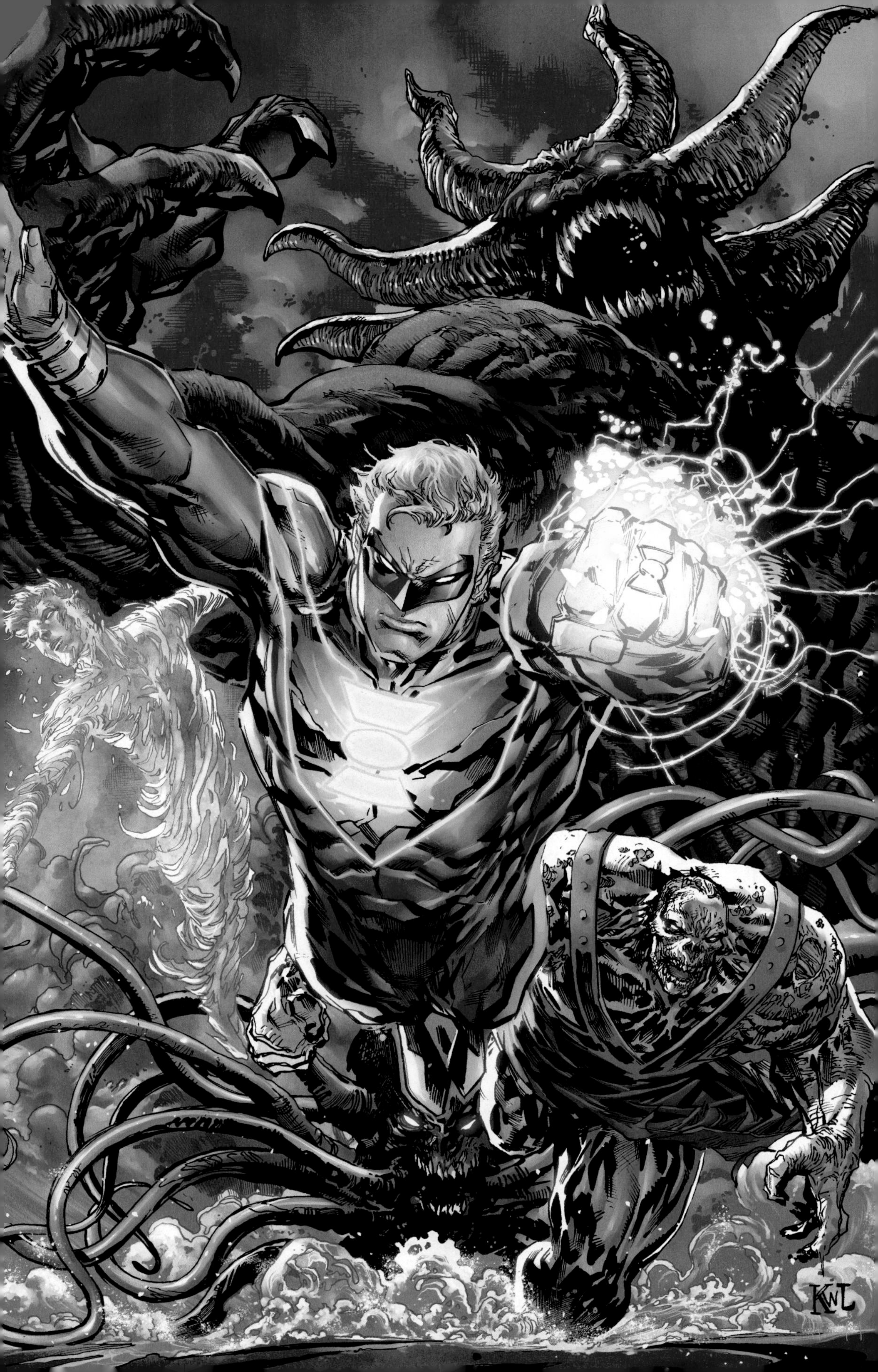

AVATARS

MARGUERITE BENNETT, MIKE JOHNSON writers **ANDY SMITH, TREVOR SCOTT, TYLER KIRKHAM, CLIFF RICHARDS, THONY SILAS** artists **PETER PANTAZIS** colorist **DEZI SIENTY** letterer cover by **KEN LASHLEY** and **TOMEU MOREY**

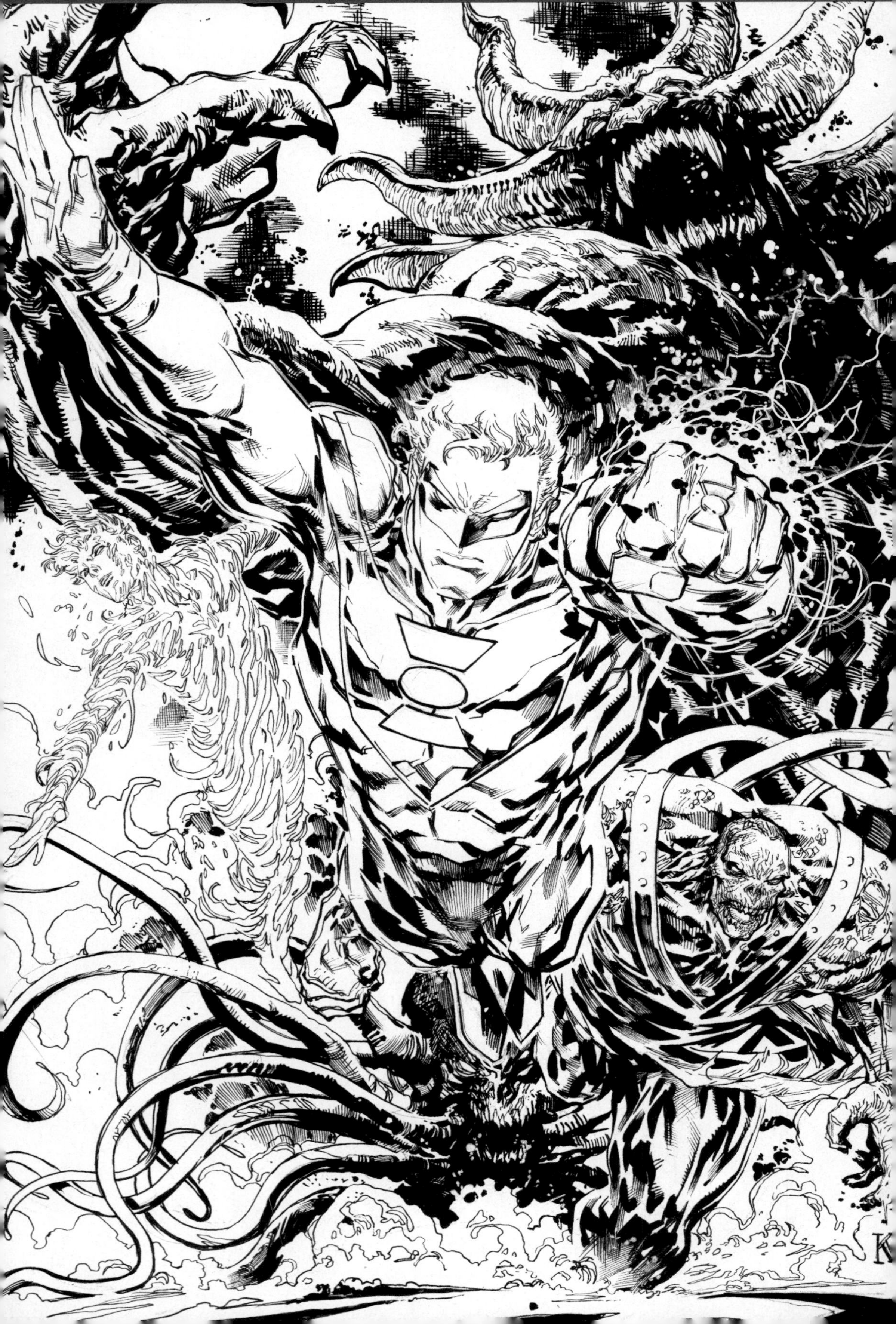

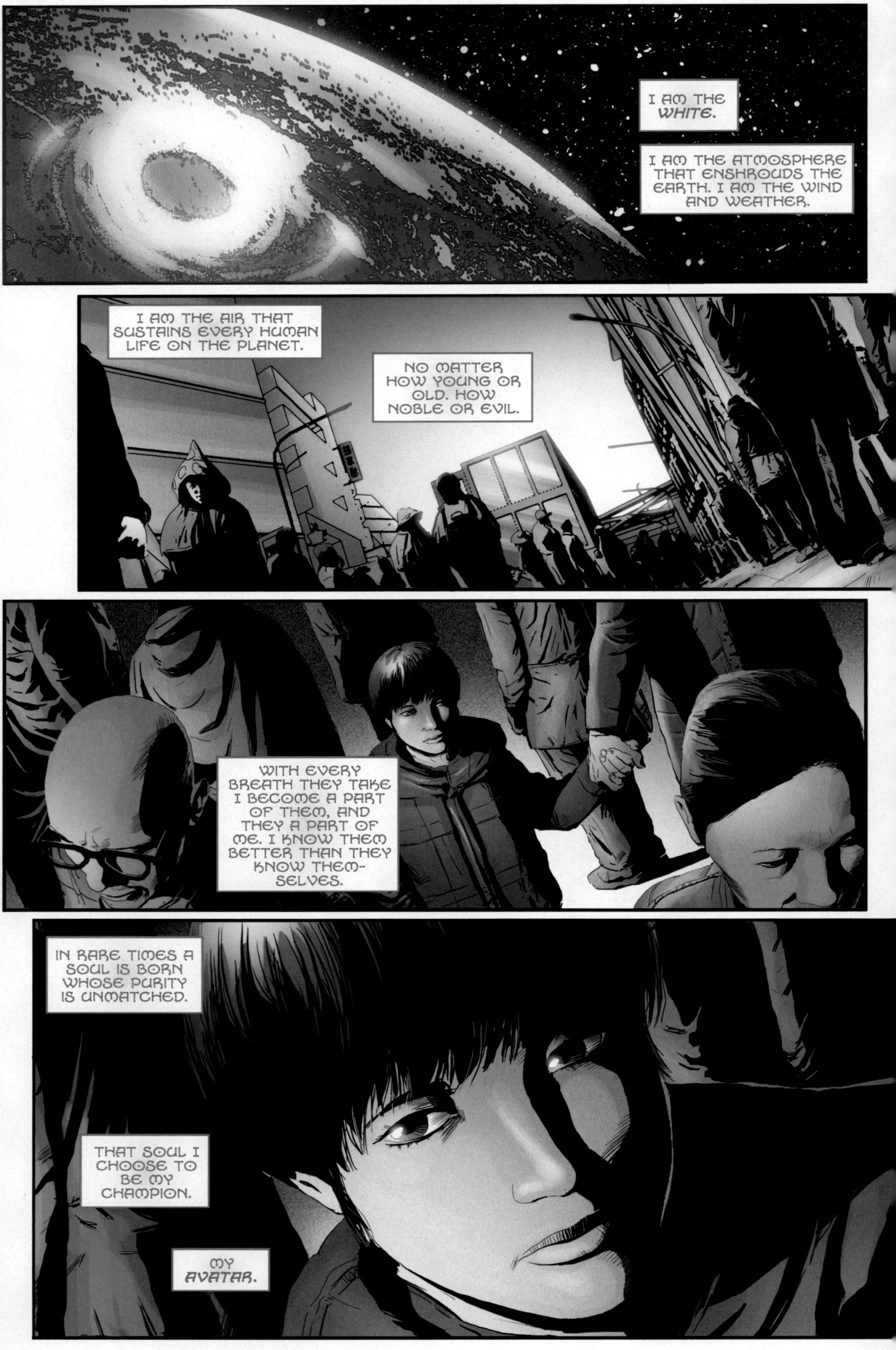
I AM THE WHITE.
I AM THE ATMOSPHERE THAT ENSHROUDS THE EARTH. I AM THE WIND AND WEATHER.
I AM THE AIR THAT SUSTAINS EVERY HUMAN LIFE ON THE PLANET.
NO MATTER HOW YOUNG OR OLD. HOW NOBLE OR EVIL.
WITH EVERY BREATH THEY TAKE I BECOME A PART OF THEM, AND THEY A PART OF ME. I KNOW THEM BETTER THAN THEY KNOW THEM-SELVES.
IN RARE TIMES A SOUL IS BORN WHOSE PURITY IS UNMATCHED.
THAT SOUL I CHOOSE TO BE MY CHAMPION.
MY AVATAR.

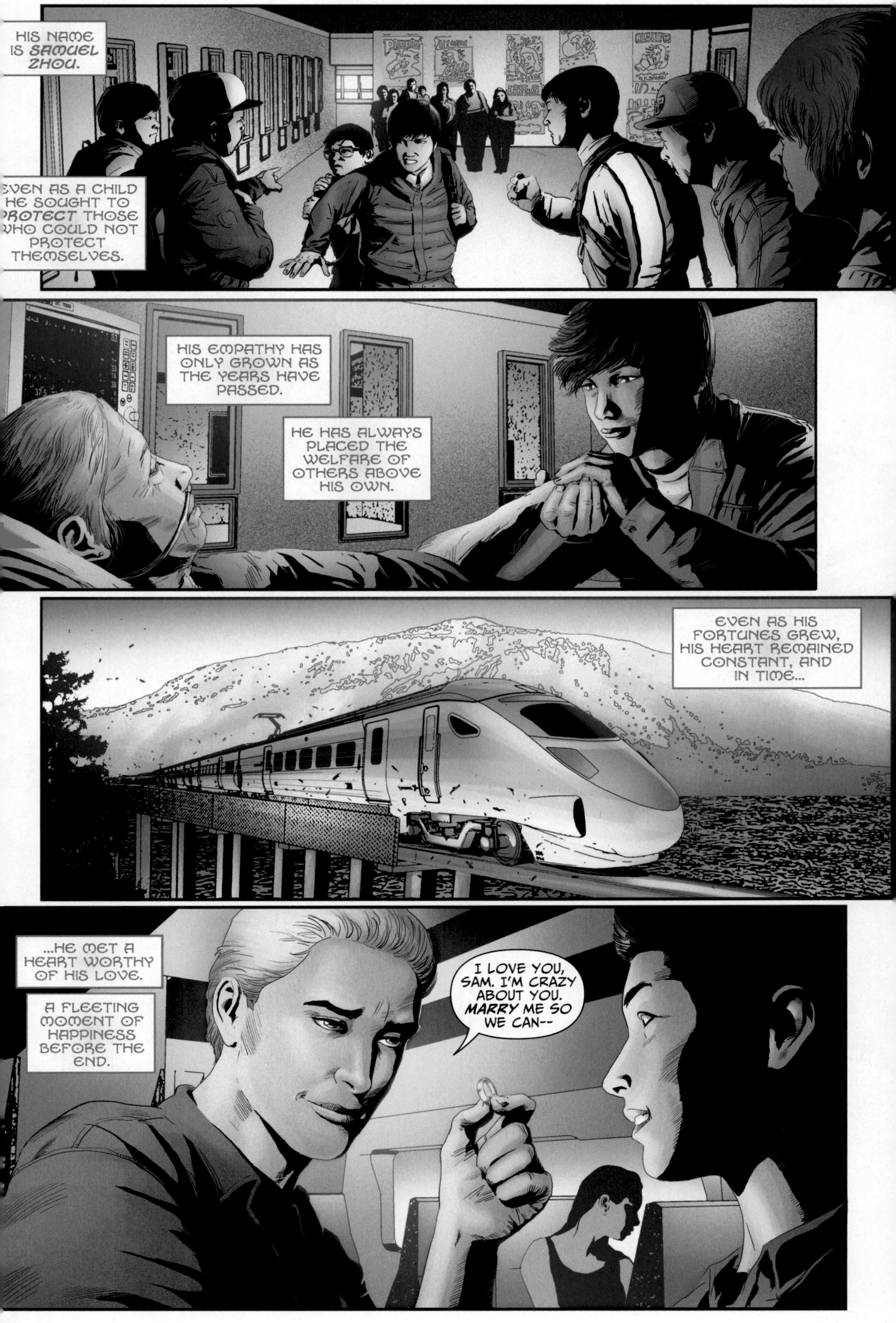
HIS NAME IS SAMUEL ZHOU.
EVEN AS A CHILD HE SOUGHT TO PROTECT THOSE WHO COULD NOT PROTECT THEMSELVES.
HIS EMPATHY HAS ONLY GROWN AS THE YEARS HAVE PASSED.
HE HAS ALWAYS PLACED THE WELFARE OF OTHERS ABOVE HIS OWN.
EVEN AS HIS FORTUNES GREW, HIS HEART REMAINED CONSTANT, AND IN TIME...
...HE MET A HEART WORTHY OF HIS LOVE.
A FLEETING MOMENT OF HAPPINESS BEFORE THE END.
I LOVE YOU, SAM. I'M CRAZY ABOUT YOU. MARRY ME SO WE CAN--

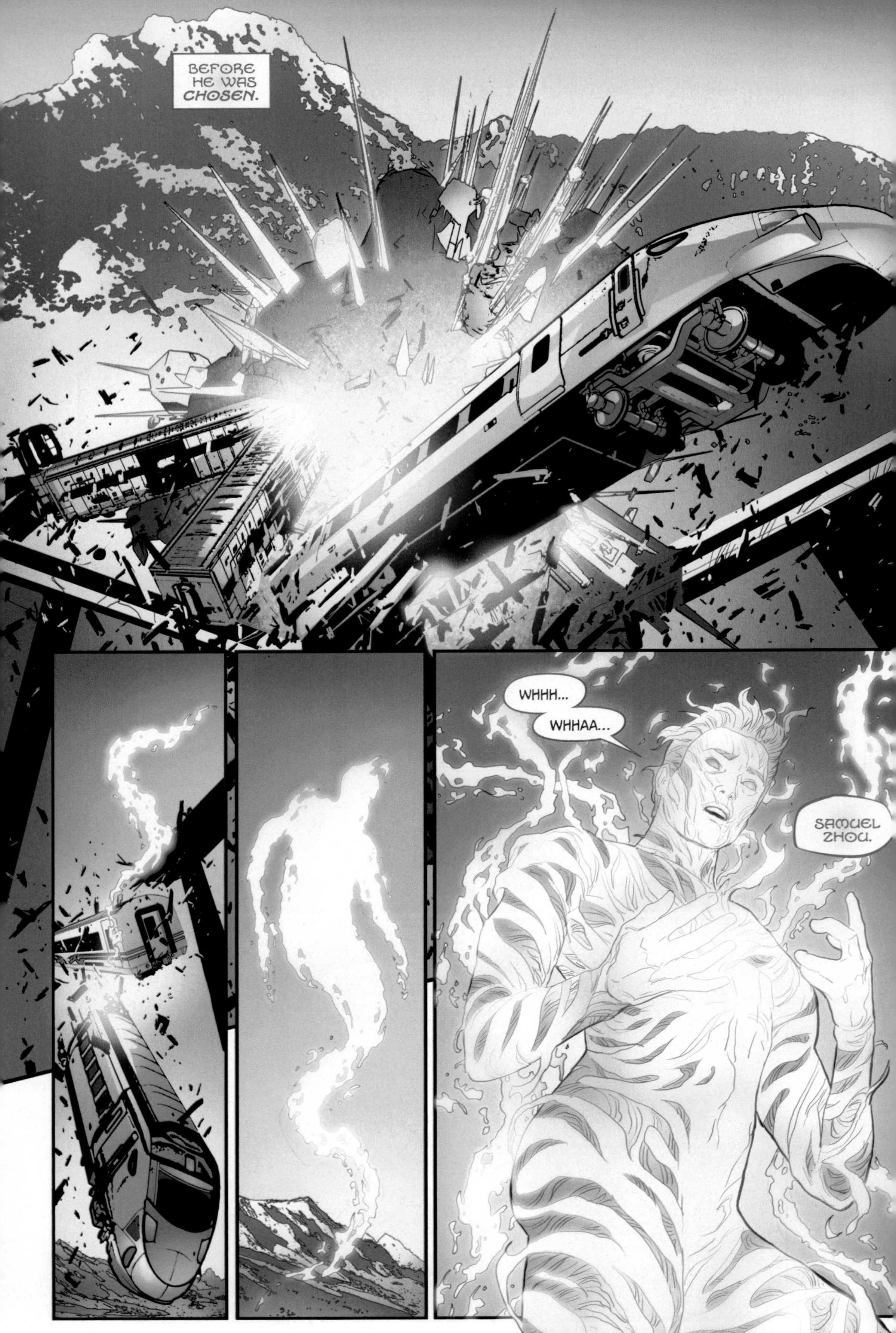
BEFORE HE WAS CHOSEN.
WHHH...
WHHAA...
SAMUEL ZHOU.

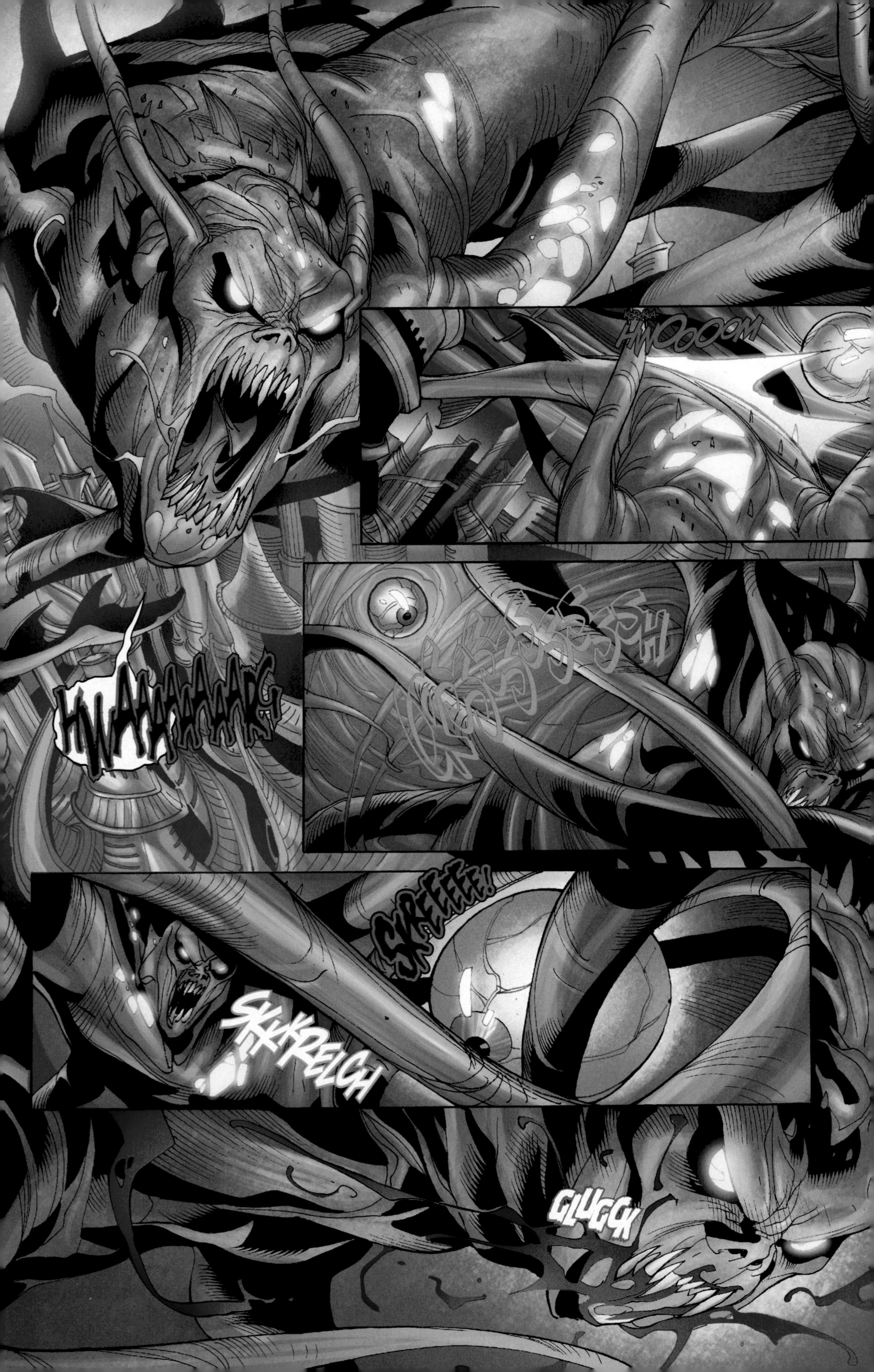
KRAKA-
HWOOOOM
HWAAAAAAARG!
SKREEEEE!
SKKKRELCH
GLUGGK

YOLANDA.
MONTEZ.

WHAM

THAT'S MY NAME.

IT DOESN'T START WITH *B*, OR *S*, OR *C*, YOU SNOTSUCKING WASTE OF VIABLE HUMAN ORGANS.

AND DON'T YOU COME NEAR MY BROTHER AGAIN.

OH, ALEJANDRO, HE GOT YOU RIGHT IN THE LIP--

YOU KNOW, I THINK YOU SHOULD RECONSIDER HIS OFFER TO TAKE YOU TO THE MOVIES. DIDN'T YOU HEAR HIM SAY HOW NICE A GUY HE WAS?

ANY MAN WHO HAS TO SAY HE'S NICE AIN'T A NICE MAN, HERMANITO.

HERMANITO, SHE SAYS! WITH THAT RED HAIR!

YOUR MOTHER AND MINE, THEY BROUGHT US INTO THIS WORLD MINUTES APART. *SISTERS.* YOU ARE MY BROTHER MORE THAN MY COUSIN.

THE FIRST THING YOU EVER GRABBED WAS MY HAND.

THE FIRST WORD I EVER SAID WAS YOUR NAME.

I WILL ALWAYS PROTECT YOU.

WHETHER YOU LIKE IT OR NOT.

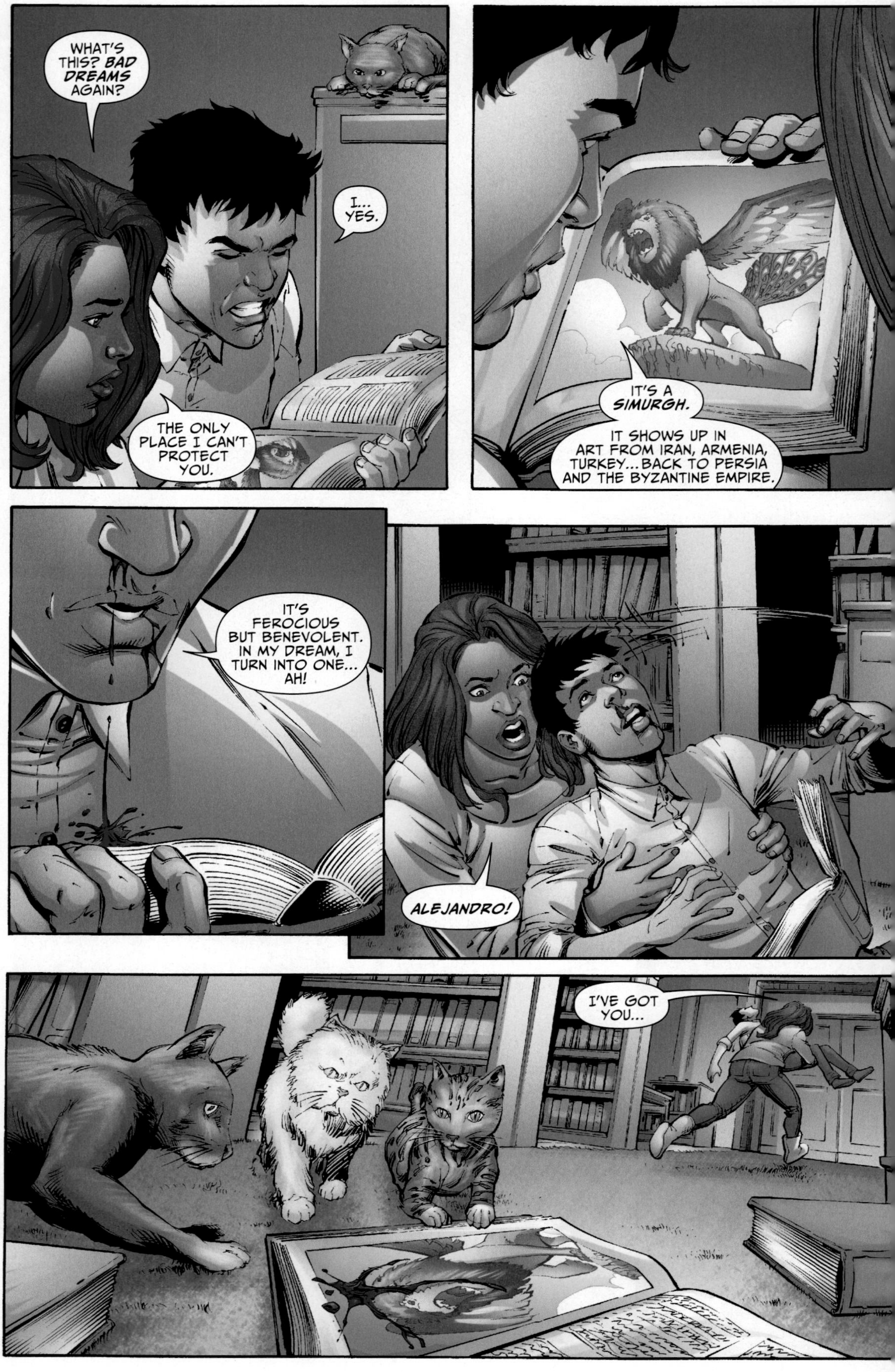
WHAT'S THIS? BAD DREAMS AGAIN?
I... YES.
THE ONLY PLACE I CAN'T PROTECT YOU.
IT'S A SIMURGH.
IT SHOWS UP IN ART FROM IRAN, ARMENIA, TURKEY... BACK TO PERSIA AND THE BYZANTINE EMPIRE.
IT'S FEROCIOUS BUT BENEVOLENT. IN MY DREAM, I TURN INTO ONE... AH!
ALEJANDRO!
I'VE GOT YOU...

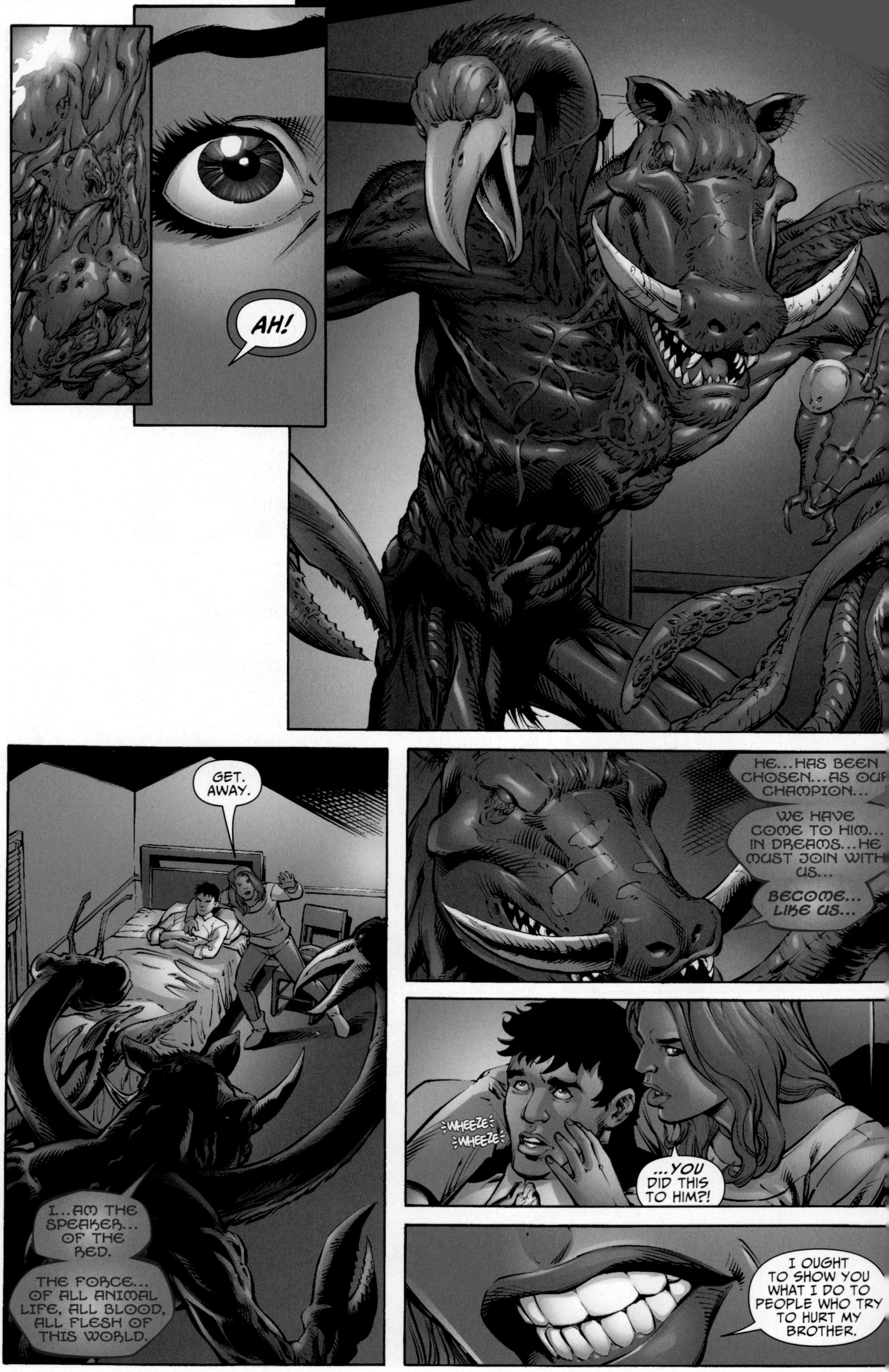

AH!
GET. AWAY.
I...AM THE SPEAKER... OF THE RED.
THE FORCE... OF ALL ANIMAL LIFE, ALL BLOOD, ALL FLESH OF THIS WORLD.
HE...HAS BEEN CHOSEN...AS OUR CHAMPION...
WE HAVE COME TO HIM... IN DREAMS...HE MUST JOIN WITH US...
BECOME... LIKE US...
WHEEZE WHEEZE
...YOU DID THIS TO HIM?!
I OUGHT TO SHOW YOU WHAT I DO TO PEOPLE WHO TRY TO HURT MY BROTHER.

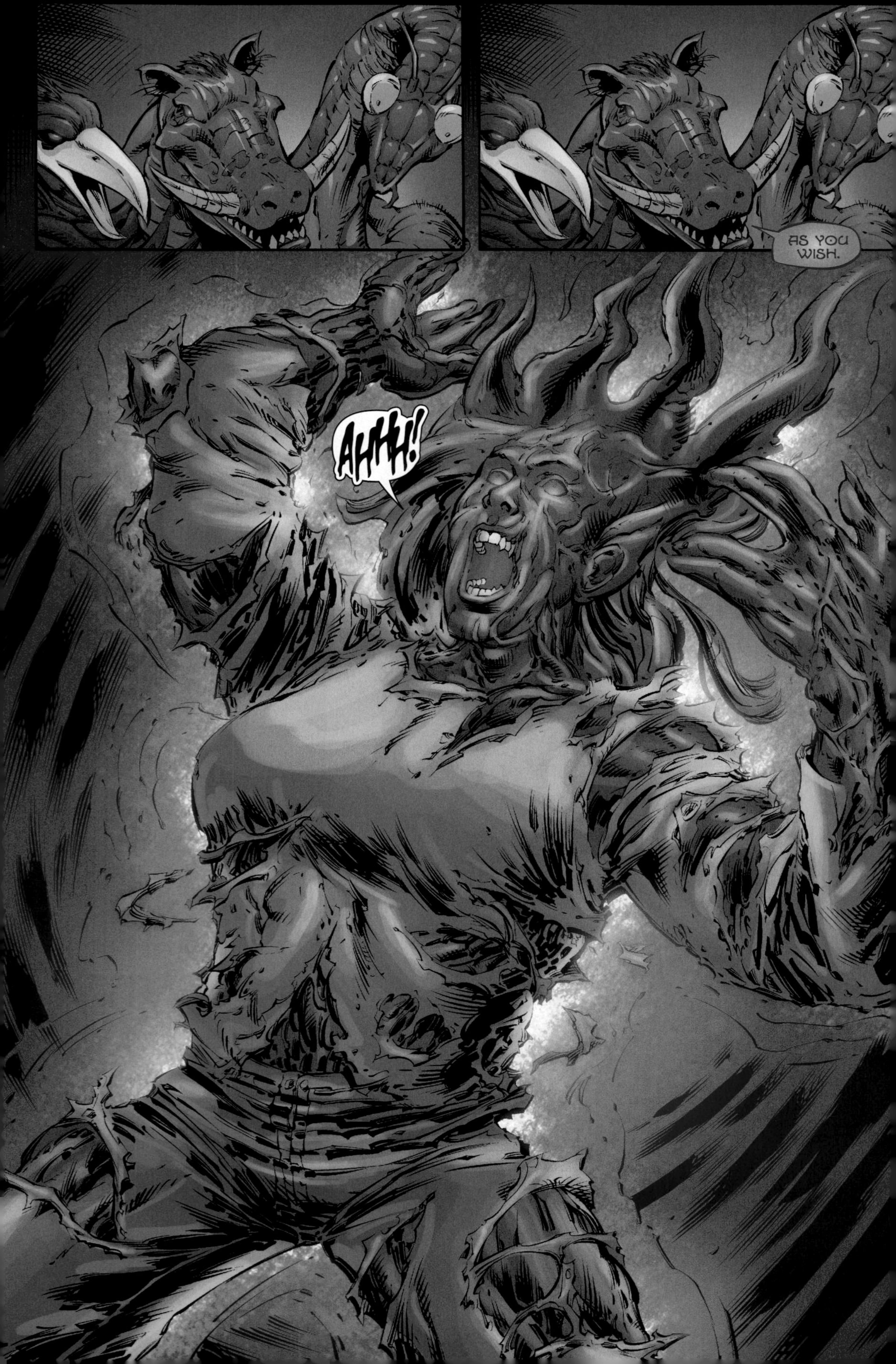
AS YOU WISH.
AHHH!

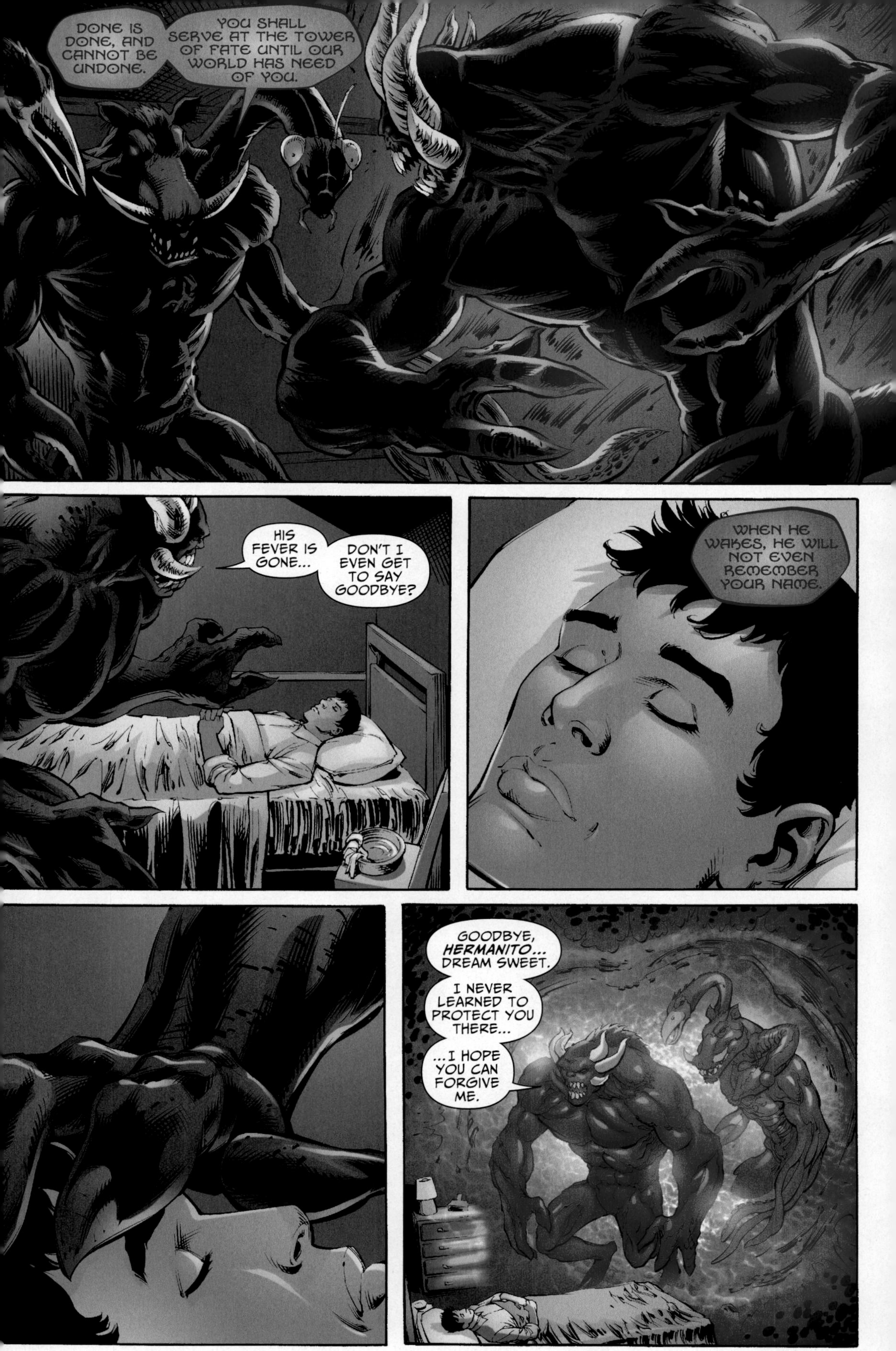
DONE IS DONE, AND CANNOT BE UNDONE.
YOU SHALL SERVE AT THE TOWER OF FATE UNTIL OUR WORLD HAS NEED OF YOU.
HIS FEVER IS GONE...
DON'T I EVEN GET TO SAY GOODBYE?
WHEN HE WAKES, HE WILL NOT EVEN REMEMBER YOUR NAME.
GOODBYE, *HERMANITO*... DREAM SWEET.
I NEVER LEARNED TO PROTECT YOU THERE...
...I HOPE YOU CAN FORGIVE ME.

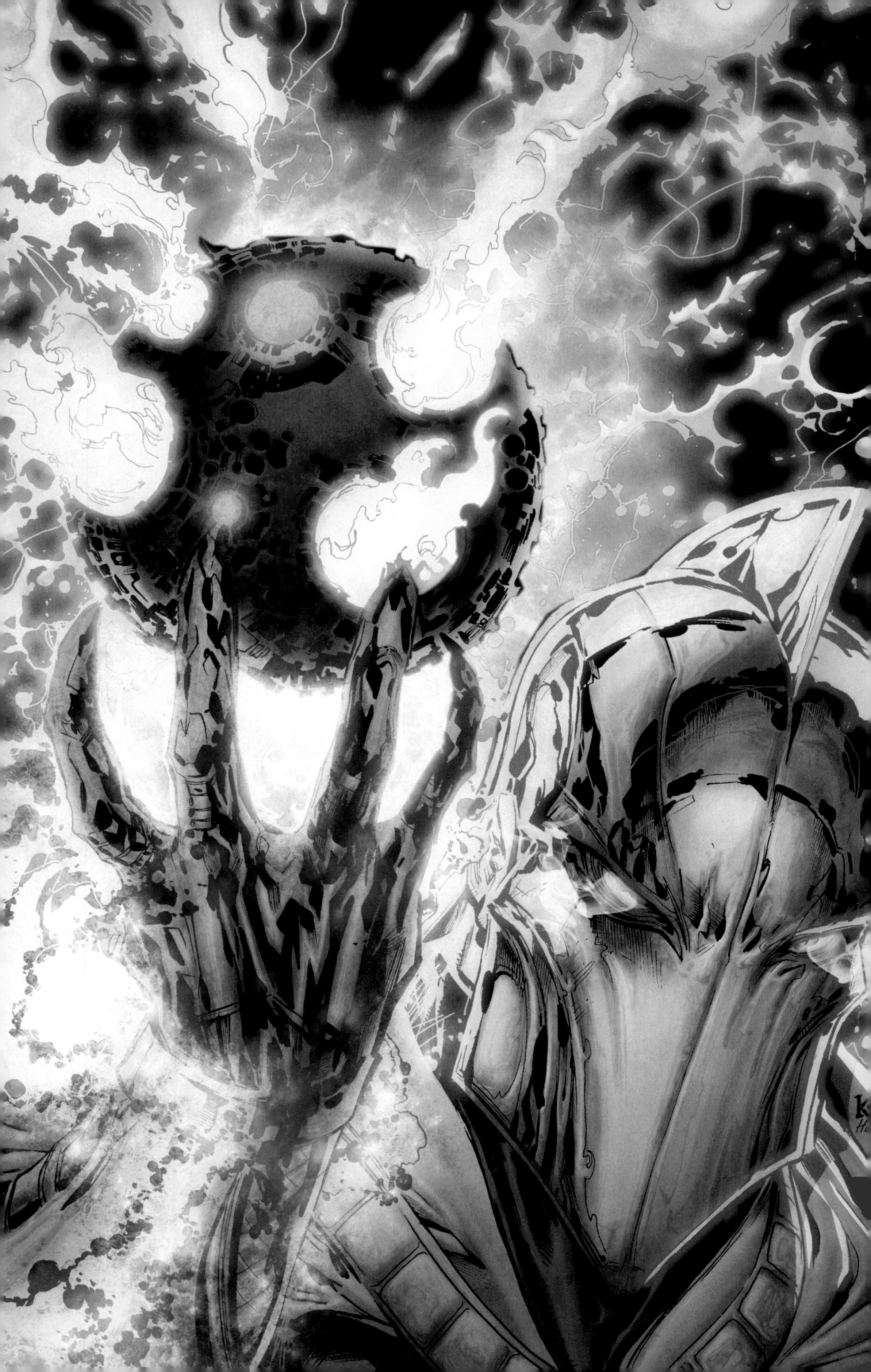

FATE & FURY

DANIEL H. WILSON, MARGUERITE BENNETT, MIKE JOHNSON writers ANDY SMITH, CLIFF RICHARDS pencillers TREVOR SCOTT, CLIFF RICHARDS inke
PETER PANTAZIS colorist TRAVIS LANHAM letterer cover by KEN LASHLEY and ANDREW DALHOUSE

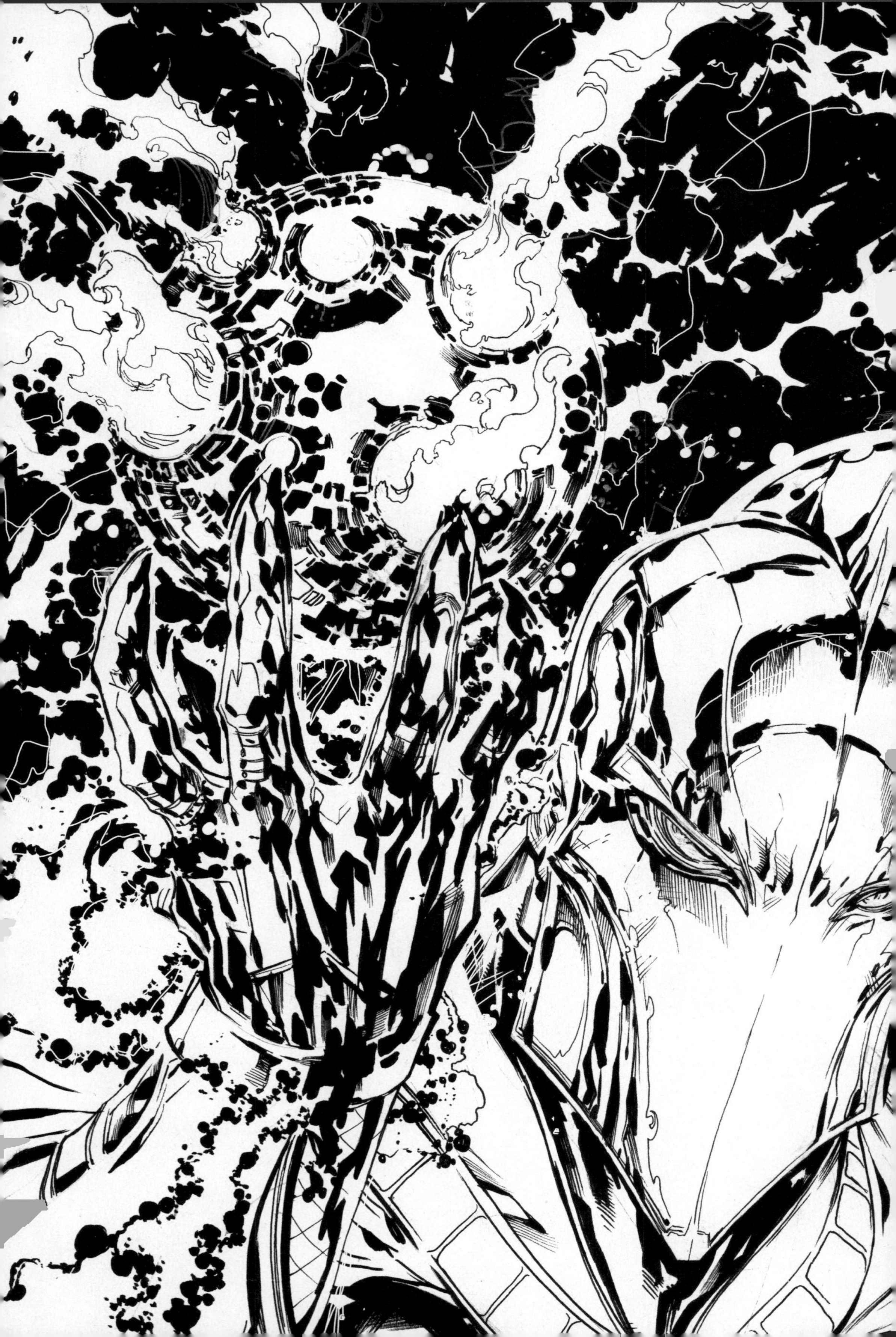

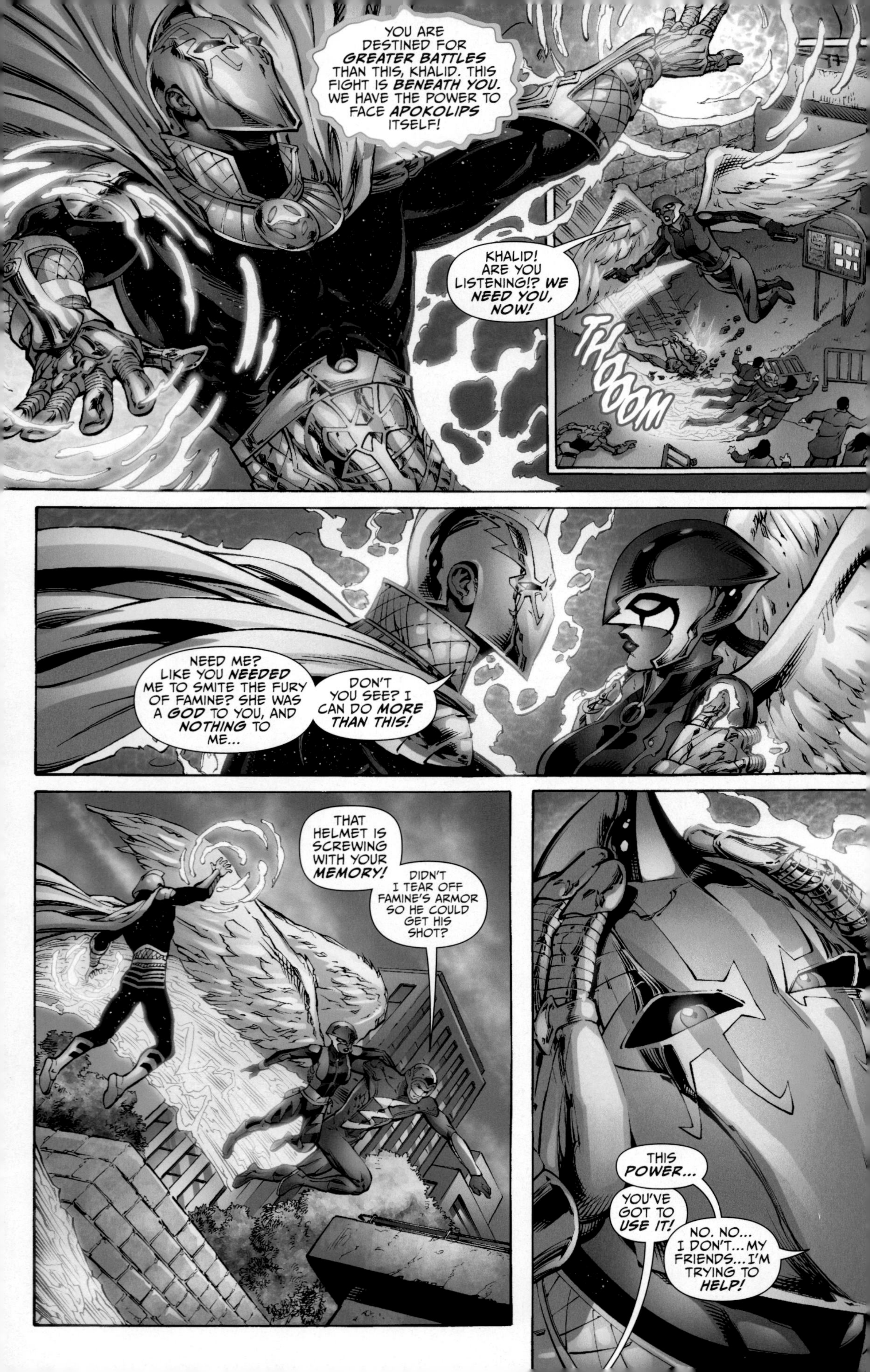
YOU ARE DESTINED FOR GREATER BATTLES THAN THIS, KHALID. THIS FIGHT IS BENEATH YOU. WE HAVE THE POWER TO FACE APOKOLIPS ITSELF!
KHALID! ARE YOU LISTENING!? WE NEED YOU, NOW!
THOOOM
NEED ME? LIKE YOU NEEDED ME TO SMITE THE FURY OF FAMINE? SHE WAS A GOD TO YOU, AND NOTHING TO ME...
DON'T YOU SEE? I CAN DO MORE THAN THIS!
THAT HELMET IS SCREWING WITH YOUR MEMORY!
DIDN'T I TEAR OFF FAMINE'S ARMOR SO HE COULD GET HIS SHOT?
THIS POWER...
YOU'VE GOT TO USE IT!
NO. NO... I DON'T... MY FRIENDS... I'M TRYING TO HELP!

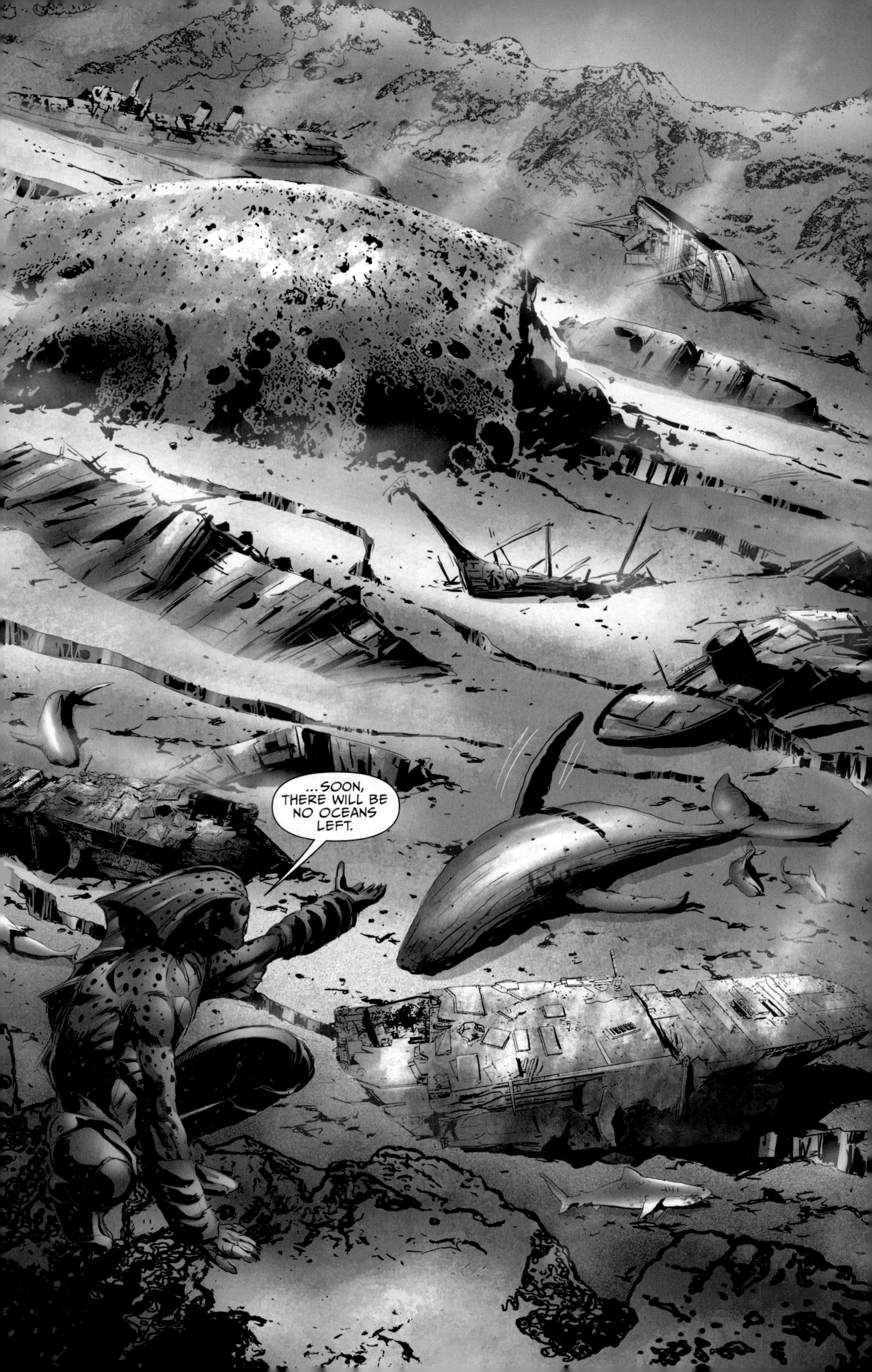
...SOON, THERE WILL BE NO OCEANS LEFT.

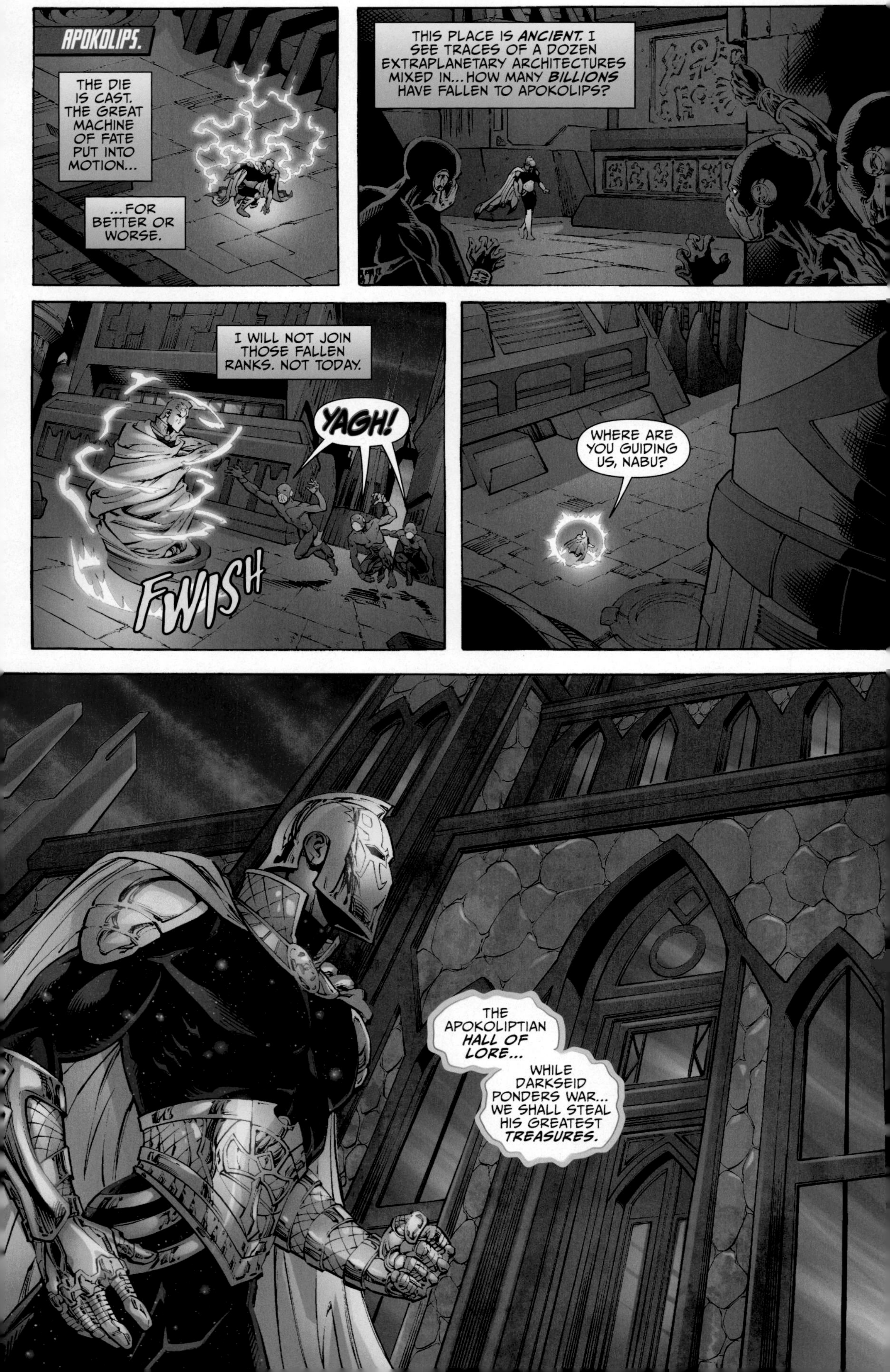
APOKOLIPS.
THE DIE IS CAST. THE GREAT MACHINE OF FATE PUT INTO MOTION...
...FOR BETTER OR WORSE.
THIS PLACE IS ANCIENT. I SEE TRACES OF A DOZEN EXTRAPLANETARY ARCHITECTURES MIXED IN... HOW MANY BILLIONS HAVE FALLEN TO APOKOLIPS?
I WILL NOT JOIN THOSE FALLEN RANKS. NOT TODAY.
YAGH!
FWISH
WHERE ARE YOU GUIDING US, NABU?
THE APOKOLIPTIAN HALL OF LORE...
WHILE DARKSEID PONDERS WAR... WE SHALL STEAL HIS GREATEST TREASURES.

THE GREAT HALL OF LORE... FABLED REPOSITORY OF APOKOLIPS' MOST POWERFUL ARTIFACTS...

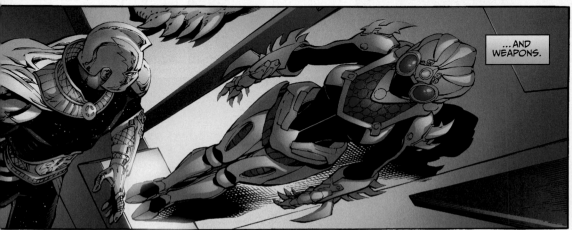

...AND WEAPONS.

THE SEAL OF A MOTHER BOX...

MANY OF THESE RELICS ARE OLDER THAN HISTORY... DESIGNED BY THOSE WHO LIVED BEFORE THE GODS THEMSELVES WERE BORN...

BUT WHAT FOUL MONSTERS OVERSEE THIS HOARD?

EMERGE, DEVIL!

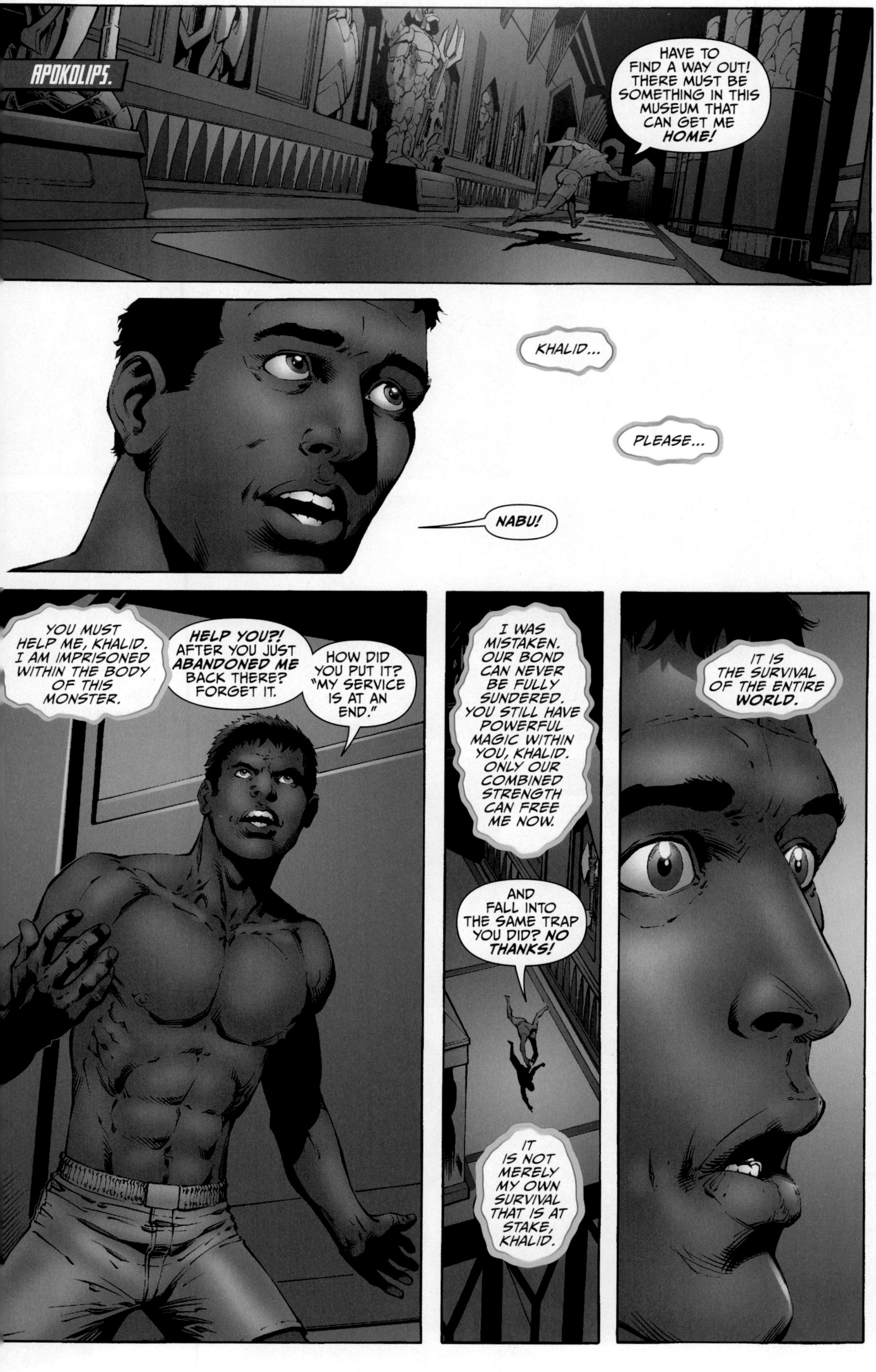
APOKOLIPS.
HAVE TO FIND A WAY OUT! THERE MUST BE SOMETHING IN THIS MUSEUM THAT CAN GET ME HOME!
KHALID...
PLEASE...
NABU!
YOU MUST HELP ME, KHALID. I AM IMPRISONED WITHIN THE BODY OF THIS MONSTER.
HELP YOU?! AFTER YOU JUST ABANDONED ME BACK THERE? FORGET IT.
HOW DID YOU PUT IT? "MY SERVICE IS AT AN END."
I WAS MISTAKEN. OUR BOND CAN NEVER BE FULLY SUNDERED. YOU STILL HAVE POWERFUL MAGIC WITHIN YOU, KHALID. ONLY OUR COMBINED STRENGTH CAN FREE ME NOW.
AND FALL INTO THE SAME TRAP YOU DID? NO THANKS!
IT IS NOT MERELY MY OWN SURVIVAL THAT IS AT STAKE, KHALID.
IT IS THE SURVIVAL OF THE ENTIRE WORLD.

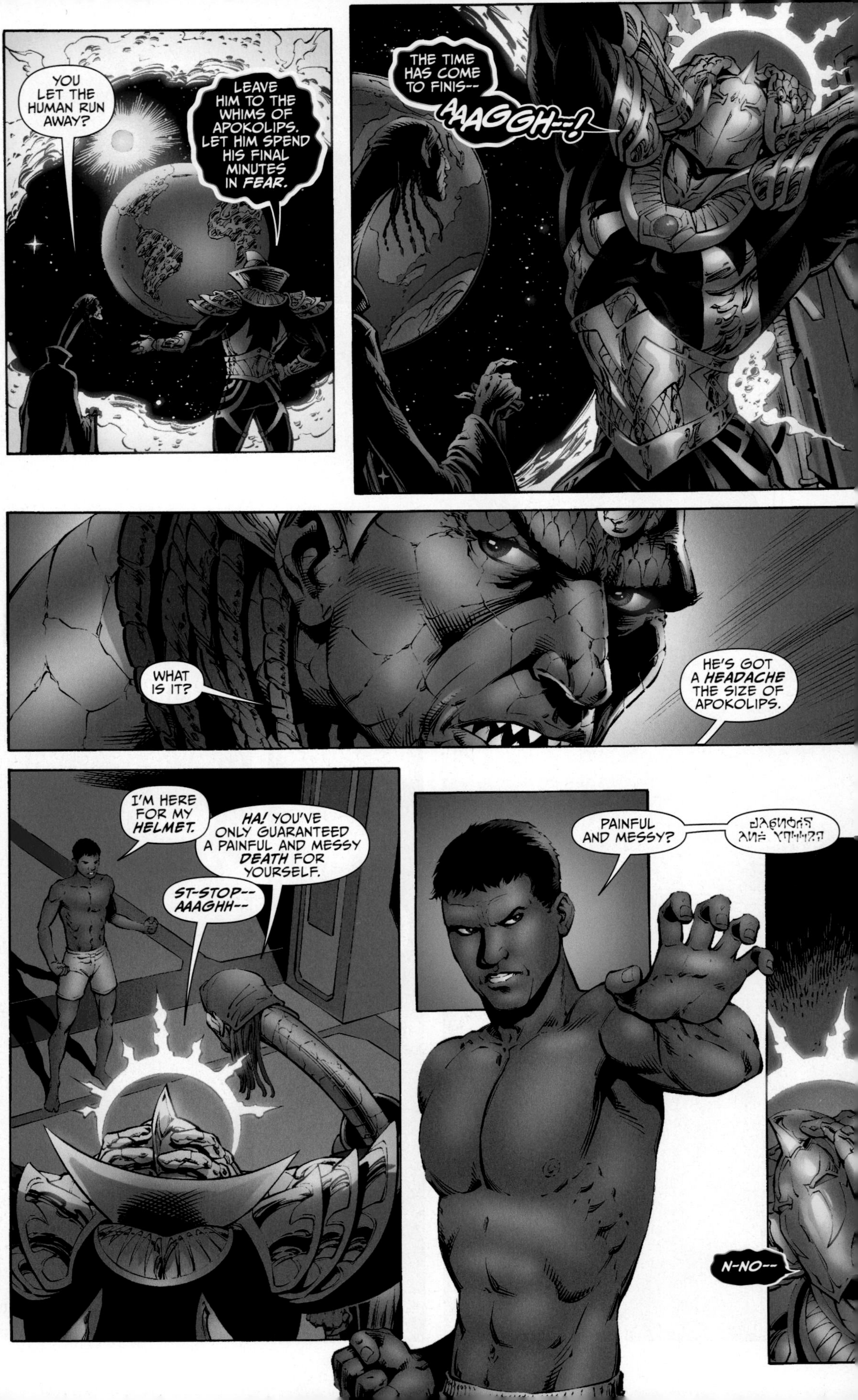
YOU LET THE HUMAN RUN AWAY?
LEAVE HIM TO THE WHIMS OF APOKOLIPS. LET HIM SPEND HIS FINAL MINUTES IN *FEAR.*
THE TIME HAS COME TO FINIS--
AAAGGH--!
WHAT IS IT?
HE'S GOT A *HEADACHE* THE SIZE OF APOKOLIPS.
I'M HERE FOR MY *HELMET.*
HA! YOU'VE ONLY GUARANTEED A PAINFUL AND MESSY *DEATH* FOR YOURSELF.
ST-STOP-- AAAGHH--
PAINFUL AND MESSY?
N-NO--

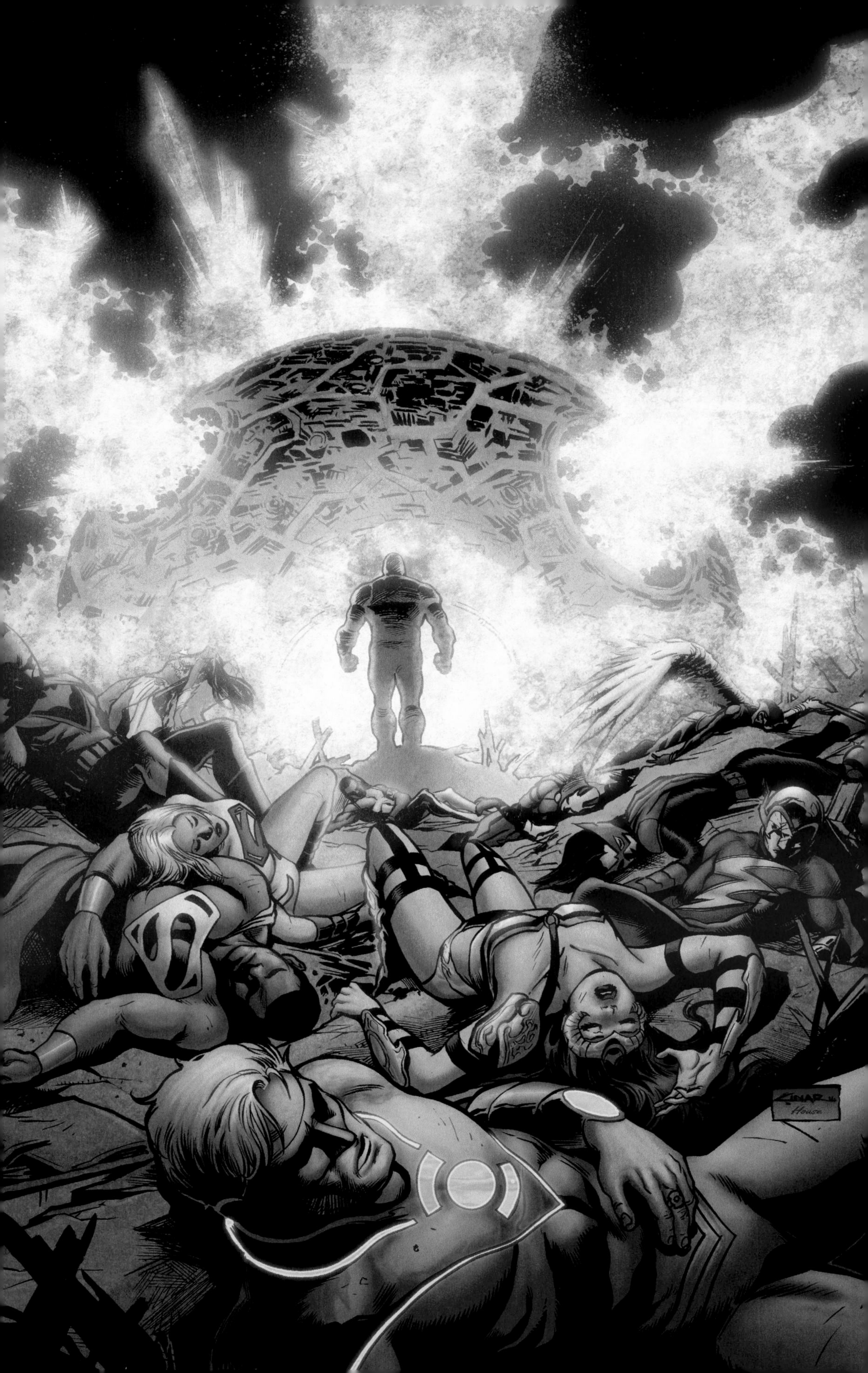
CINAR
House

GROUNDED

DANIEL H. WILSON, MARGUERITE BENNETT, MIKE JOHNSON writers ANDY SMITH, AIRI KAMIYAMA pencillers TREVOR SCOTT, AIRI KAMIYAMA inkers PETER PANTAZIS colorist TRAVIS LANHAM letterer cover by YILDIRAY CINAR and ANDREW DALHOUSE

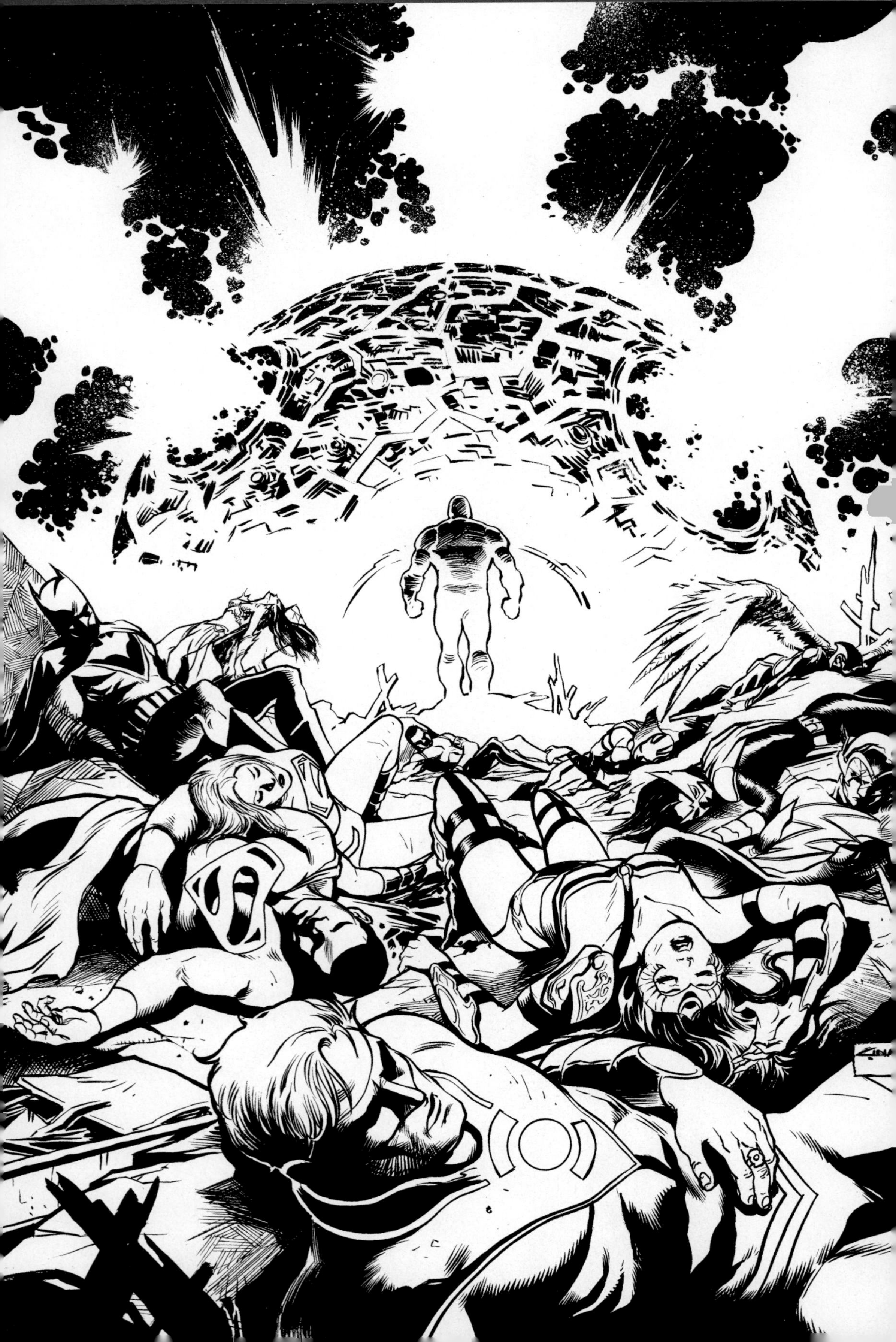

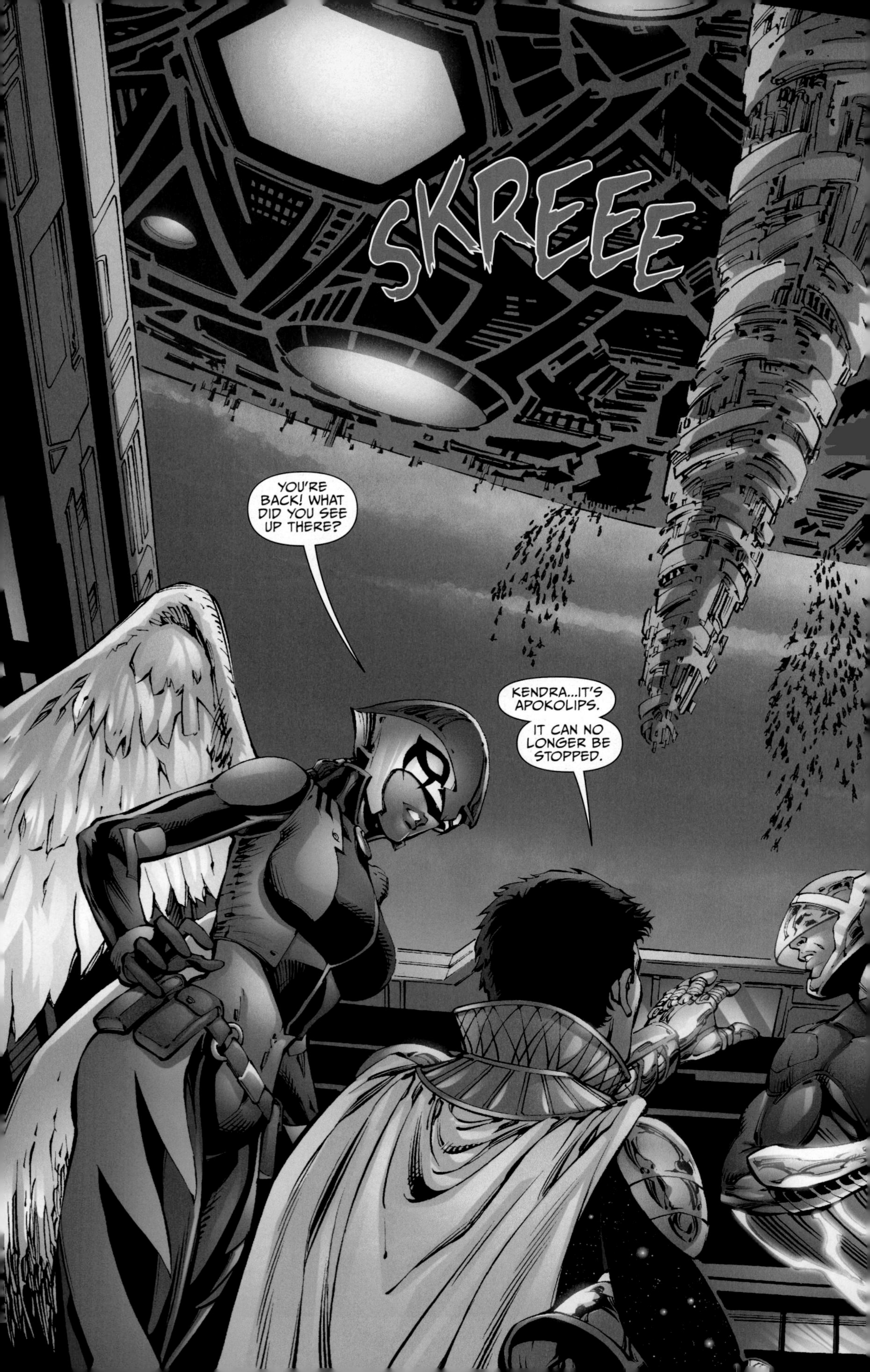
SKREEE
YOU'RE BACK! WHAT DID YOU SEE UP THERE?
KENDRA...IT'S APOKOLIPS.
IT CAN NO LONGER BE STOPPED.

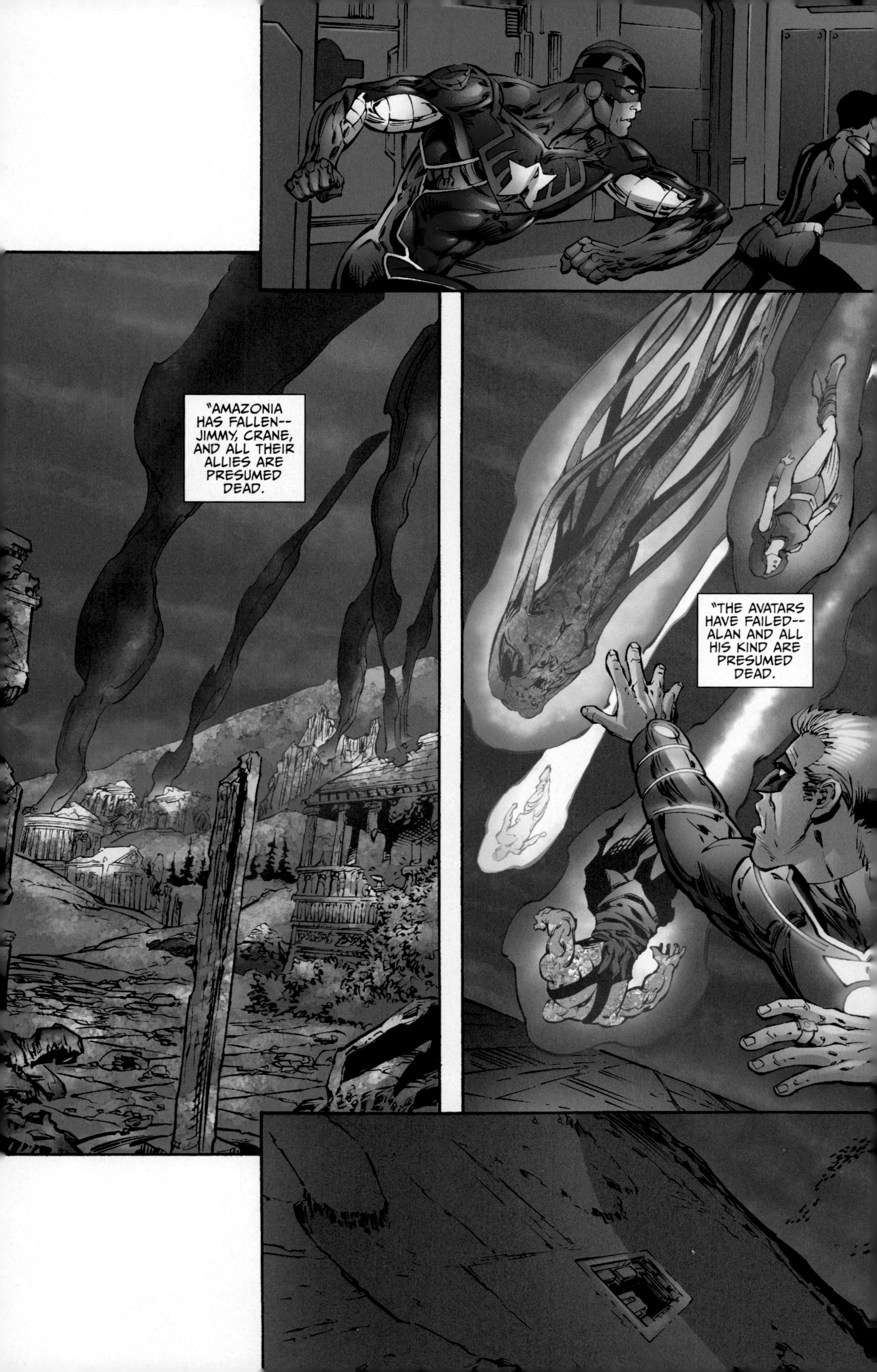
"AMAZONIA HAS FALLEN--JIMMY, CRANE, AND ALL THEIR ALLIES ARE PRESUMED DEAD.
"THE AVATARS HAVE FAILED--ALAN AND ALL HIS KIND ARE PRESUMED DEAD.

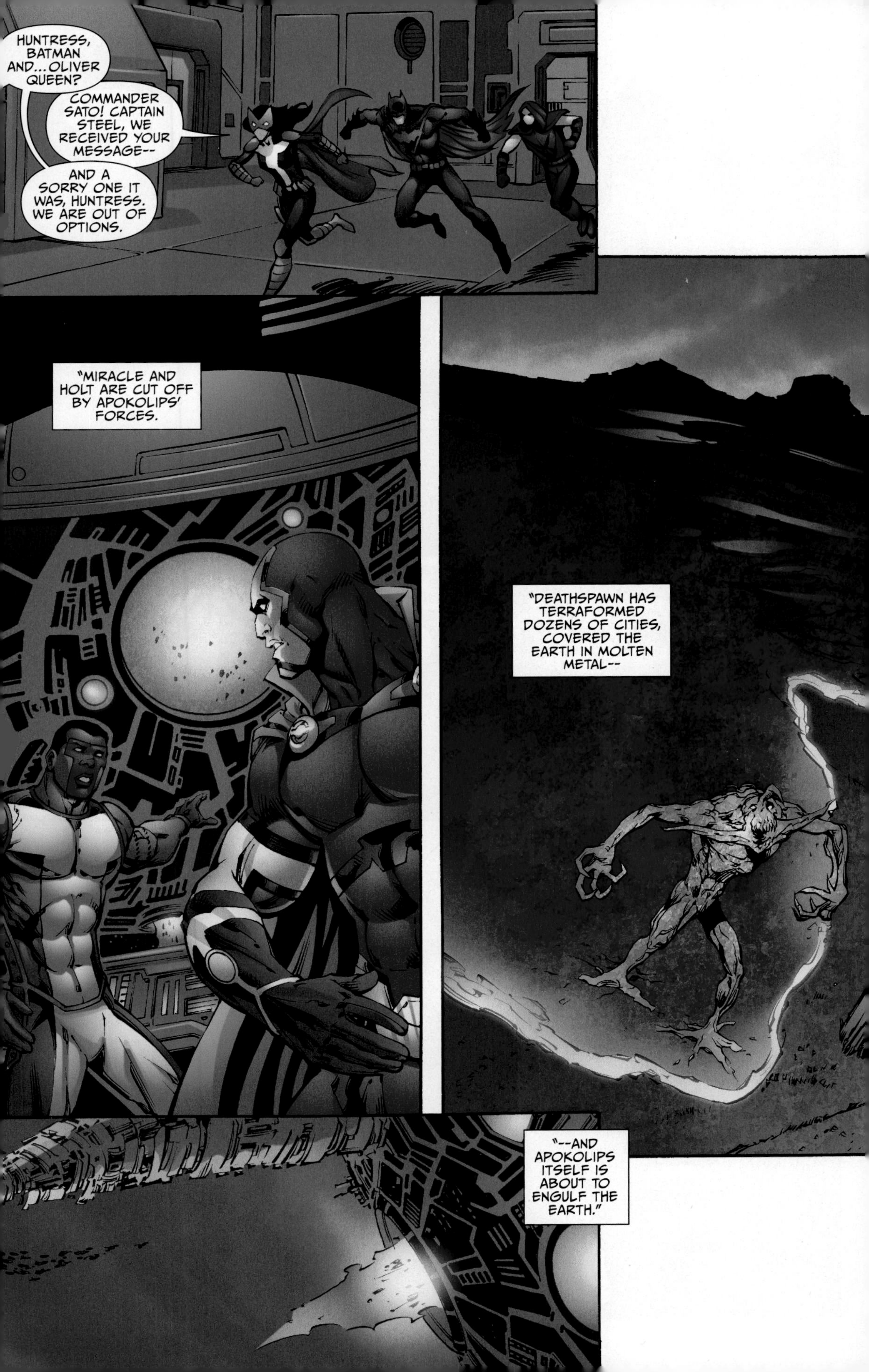

HUNTRESS, BATMAN AND...OLIVER QUEEN?
COMMANDER SATO! CAPTAIN STEEL, WE RECEIVED YOUR MESSAGE--
AND A SORRY ONE IT WAS, HUNTRESS. WE ARE OUT OF OPTIONS.
"MIRACLE AND HOLT ARE CUT OFF BY APOKOLIPS' FORCES.
"DEATHSPAWN HAS TERRAFORMED DOZENS OF CITIES, COVERED THE EARTH IN MOLTEN METAL--
"--AND APOKOLIPS ITSELF IS ABOUT TO ENGULF THE EARTH."

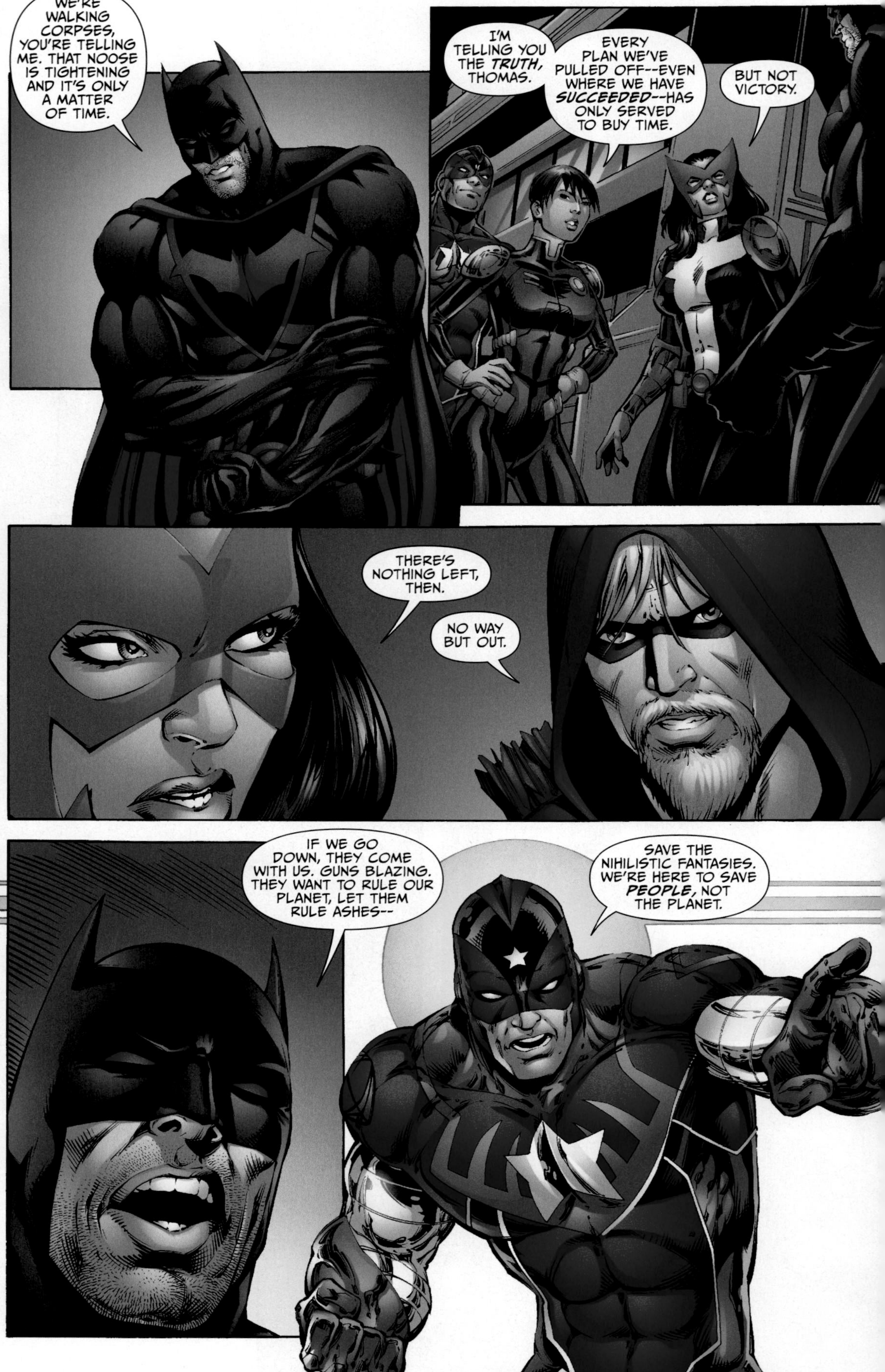
WE'RE WALKING CORPSES, YOU'RE TELLING ME. THAT NOOSE IS TIGHTENING AND IT'S ONLY A MATTER OF TIME.
I'M TELLING YOU THE TRUTH, THOMAS.
EVERY PLAN WE'VE PULLED OFF--EVEN WHERE WE HAVE SUCCEEDED--HAS ONLY SERVED TO BUY TIME.
BUT NOT VICTORY.
THERE'S NOTHING LEFT, THEN.
NO WAY BUT OUT.
IF WE GO DOWN, THEY COME WITH US. GUNS BLAZING. THEY WANT TO RULE OUR PLANET, LET THEM RULE ASHES--
SAVE THE NIHILISTIC FANTASIES. WE'RE HERE TO SAVE PEOPLE, NOT THE PLANET.

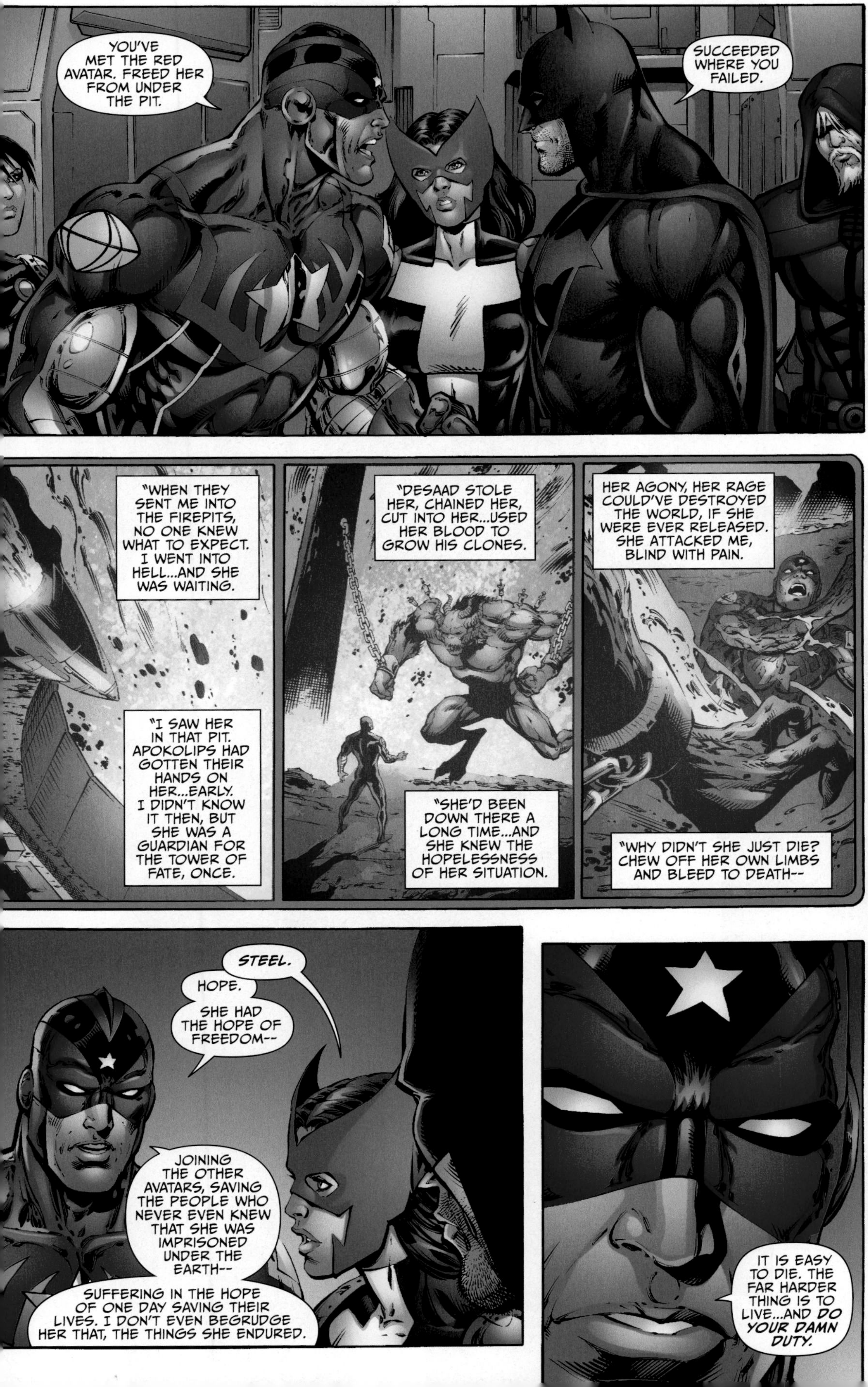

YOU'VE MET THE RED AVATAR. FREED HER FROM UNDER THE PIT.
SUCCEEDED WHERE YOU FAILED.
"WHEN THEY SENT ME INTO THE FIREPITS, NO ONE KNEW WHAT TO EXPECT. I WENT INTO HELL...AND SHE WAS WAITING.
"I SAW HER IN THAT PIT. APOKOLIPS HAD GOTTEN THEIR HANDS ON HER...EARLY. I DIDN'T KNOW IT THEN, BUT SHE WAS A GUARDIAN FOR THE TOWER OF FATE, ONCE.
"DESAAD STOLE HER, CHAINED HER, CUT INTO HER...USED HER BLOOD TO GROW HIS CLONES.
"SHE'D BEEN DOWN THERE A LONG TIME...AND SHE KNEW THE HOPELESSNESS OF HER SITUATION.
HER AGONY, HER RAGE COULD'VE DESTROYED THE WORLD, IF SHE WERE EVER RELEASED. SHE ATTACKED ME, BLIND WITH PAIN.
"WHY DIDN'T SHE JUST DIE? CHEW OFF HER OWN LIMBS AND BLEED TO DEATH--
STEEL.
HOPE.
SHE HAD THE HOPE OF FREEDOM--
JOINING THE OTHER AVATARS, SAVING THE PEOPLE WHO NEVER EVEN KNEW THAT SHE WAS IMPRISONED UNDER THE EARTH--
SUFFERING IN THE HOPE OF ONE DAY SAVING THEIR LIVES. I DON'T EVEN BEGRUDGE HER THAT, THE THINGS SHE ENDURED.
IT IS EASY TO DIE. THE FAR HARDER THING IS TO LIVE...AND DO YOUR DAMN DUTY.

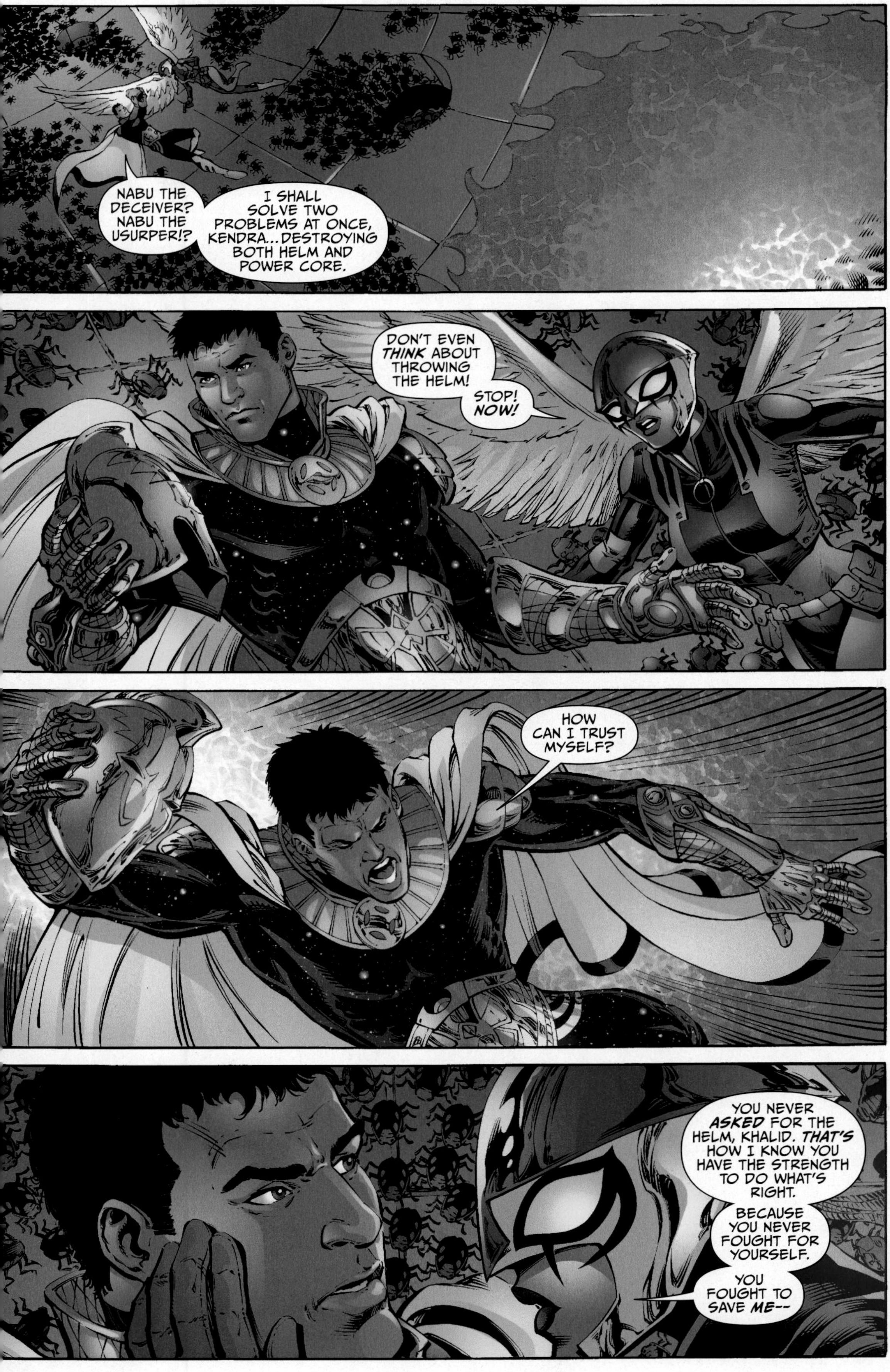
NABU THE DECEIVER? NABU THE USURPER!?
I SHALL SOLVE TWO PROBLEMS AT ONCE, KENDRA...DESTROYING BOTH HELM AND POWER CORE.
DON'T EVEN THINK ABOUT THROWING THE HELM!
STOP! NOW!
HOW CAN I TRUST MYSELF?
YOU NEVER ASKED FOR THE HELM, KHALID. THAT'S HOW I KNOW YOU HAVE THE STRENGTH TO DO WHAT'S RIGHT.
BECAUSE YOU NEVER FOUGHT FOR YOURSELF.
YOU FOUGHT TO SAVE ME--

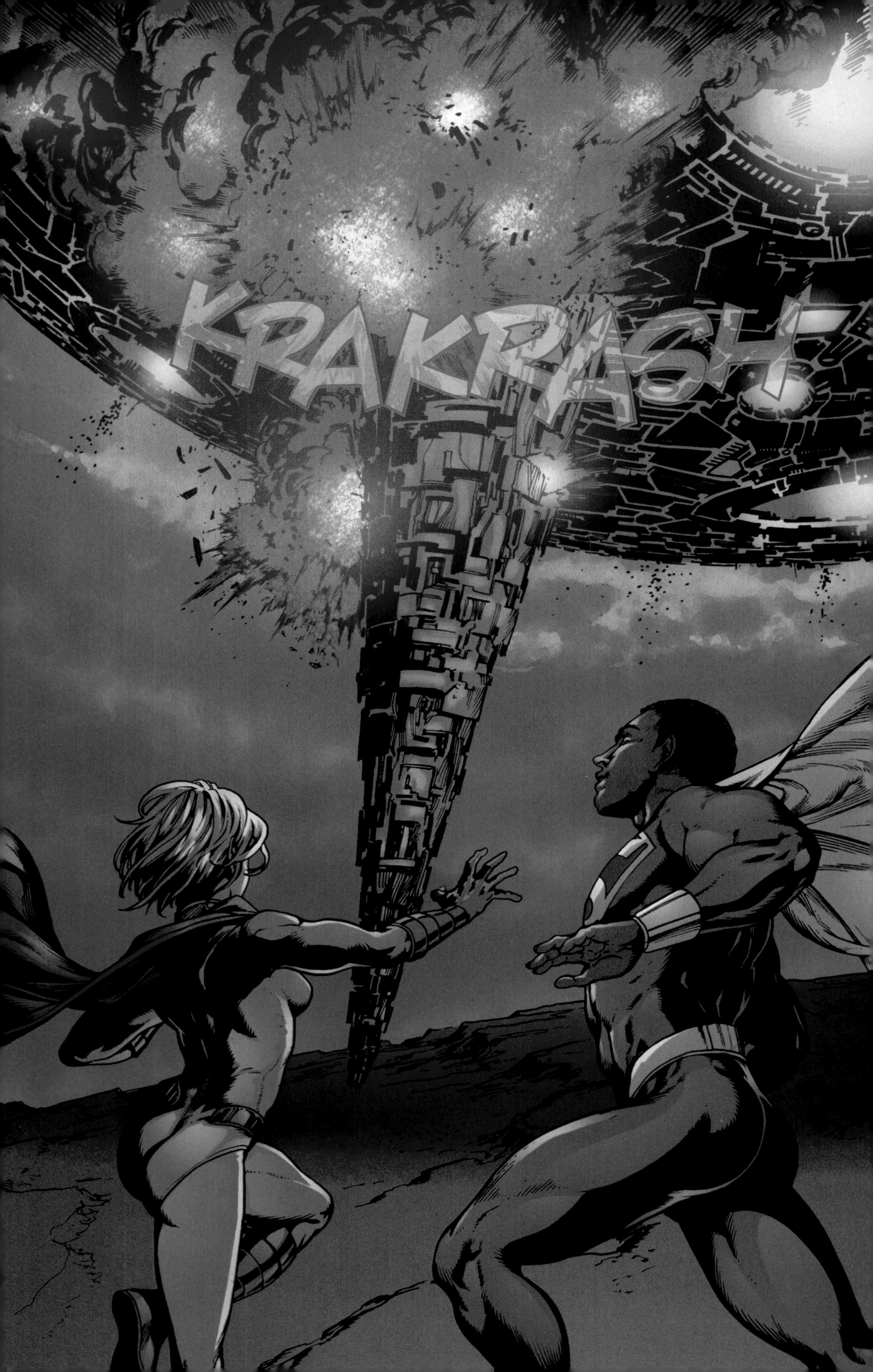
KRAKRASH!

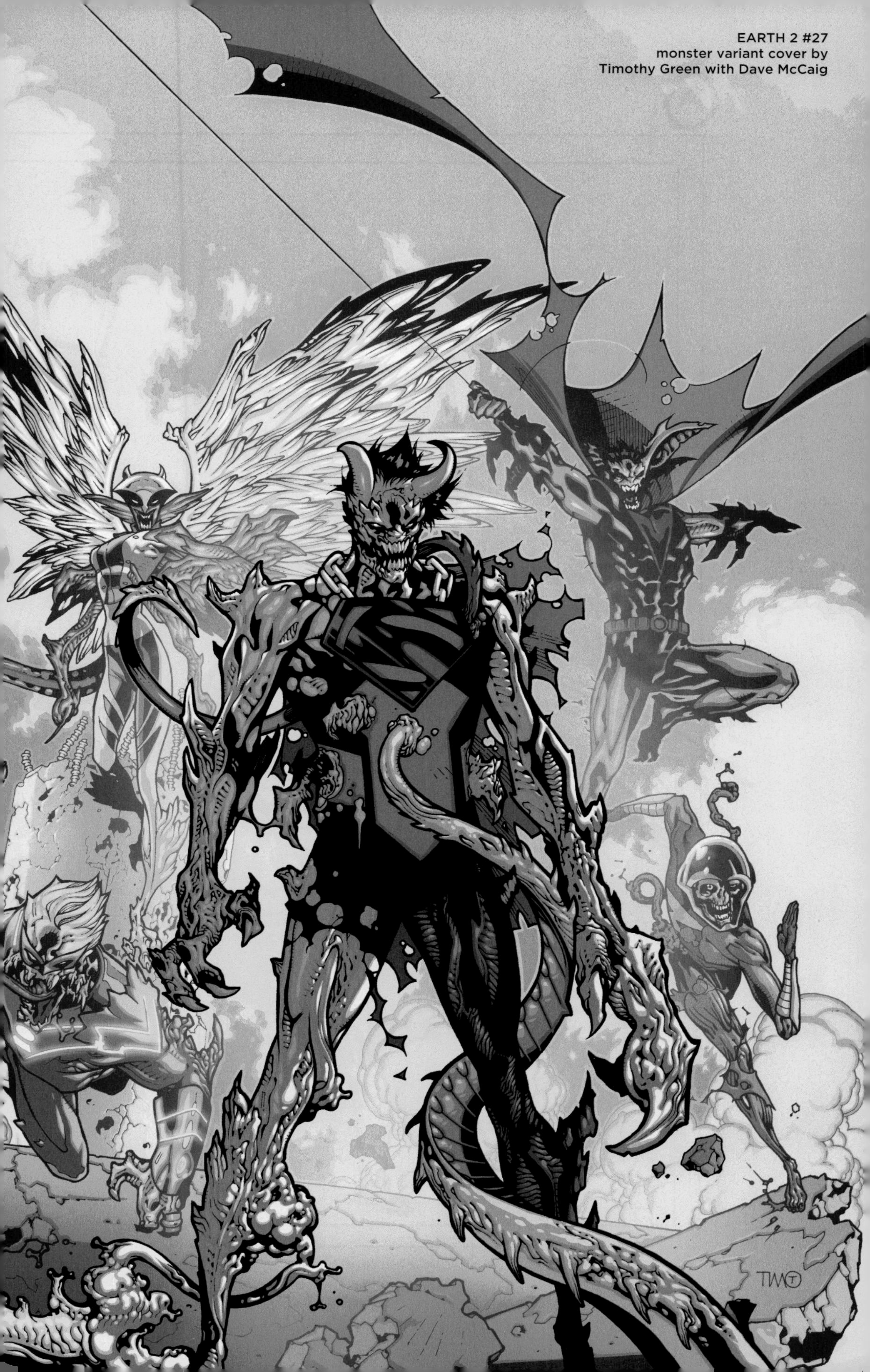

EARTH 2 #27
monster variant cover by
Timothy Green with Dave McCaig

A

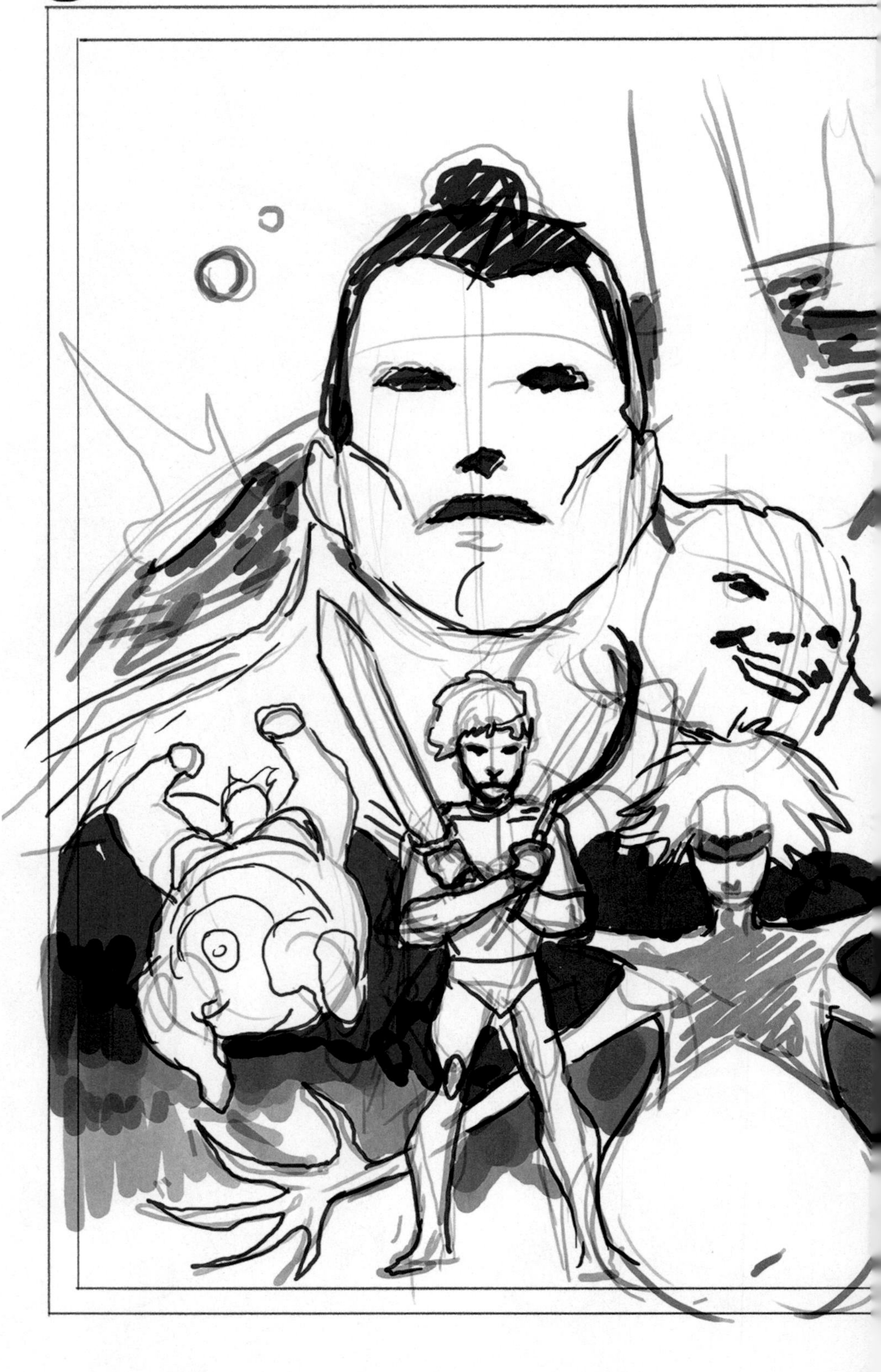

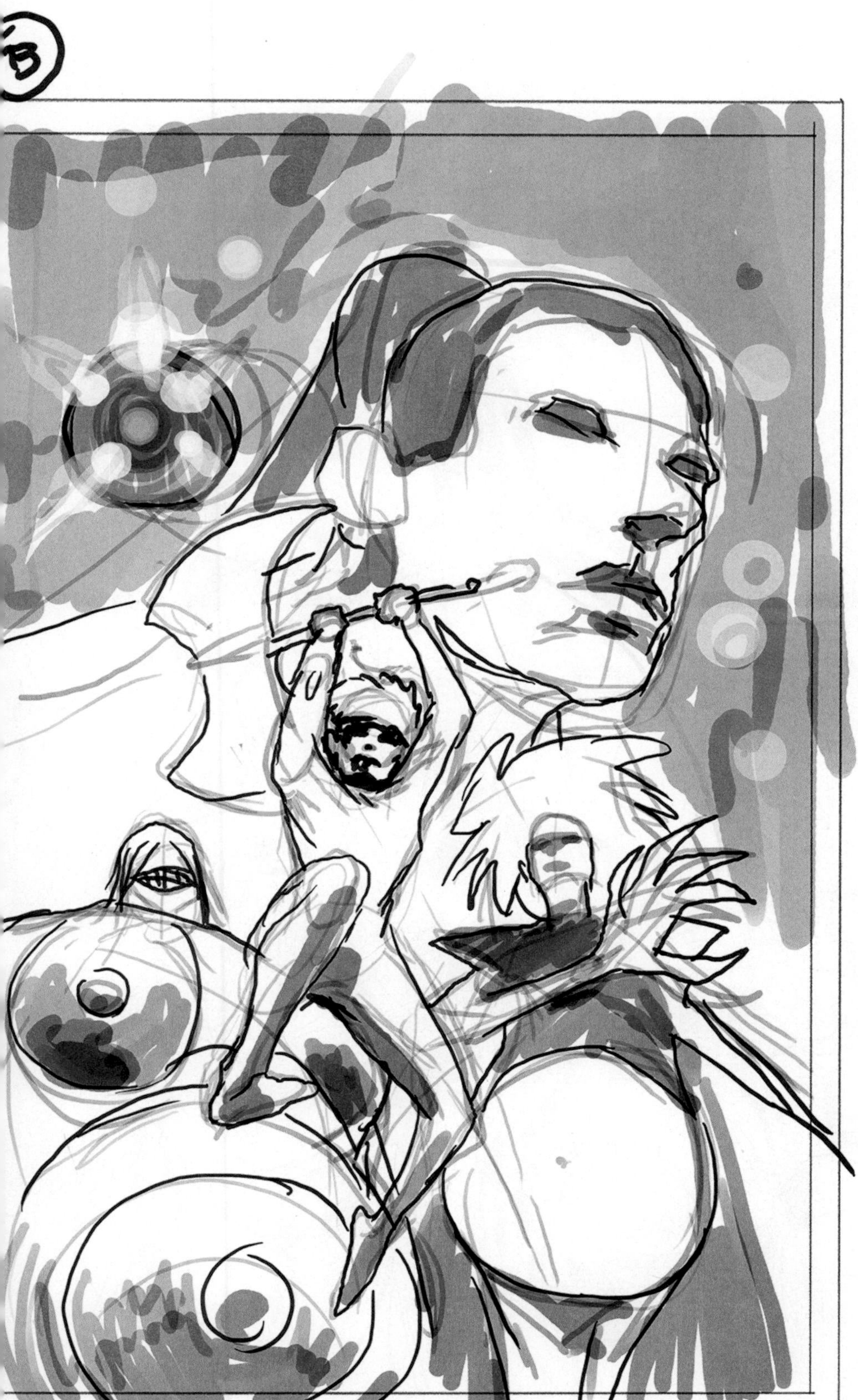
B

EARTH 2 #28 cover sketches
by Stephen Segovia

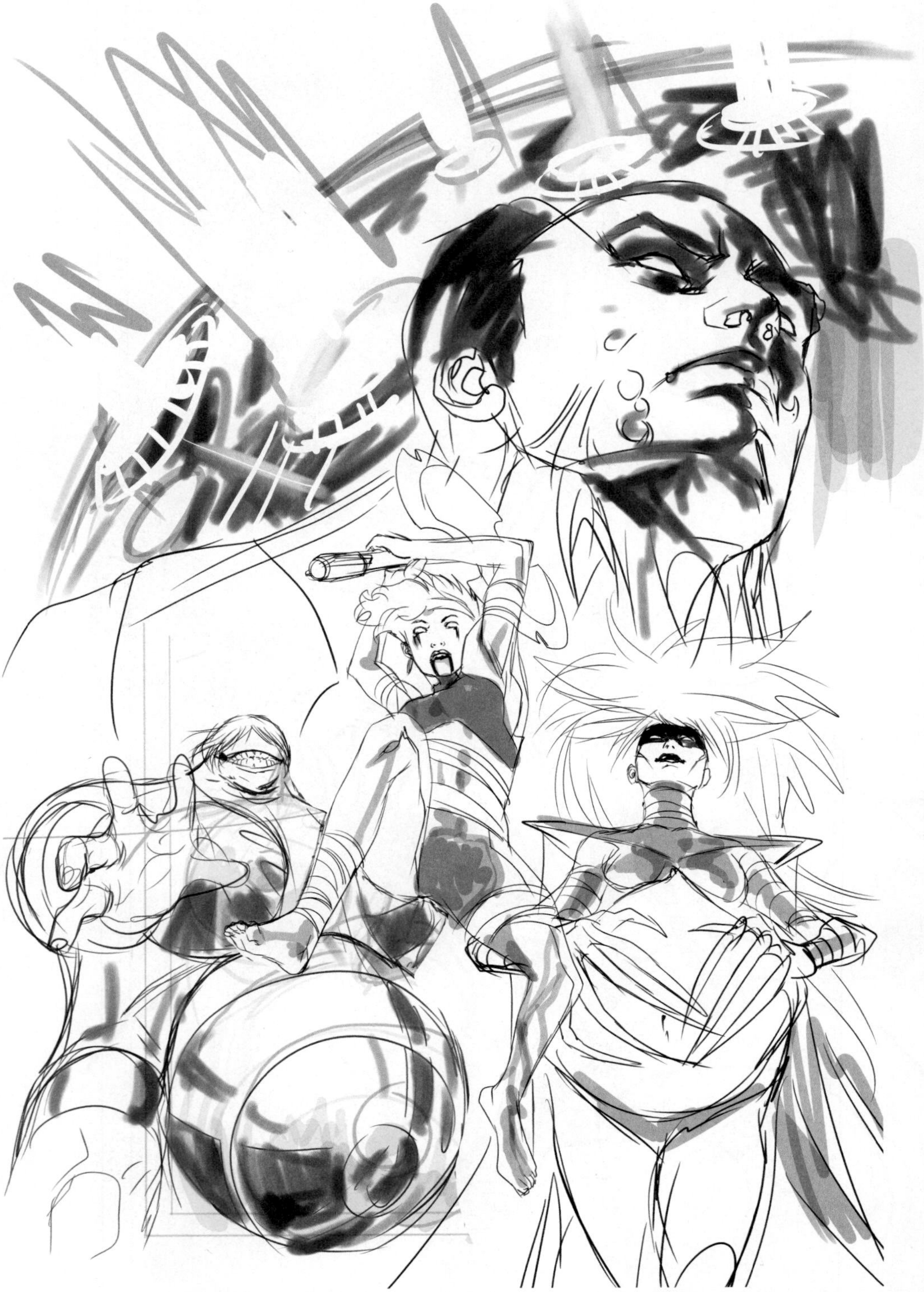

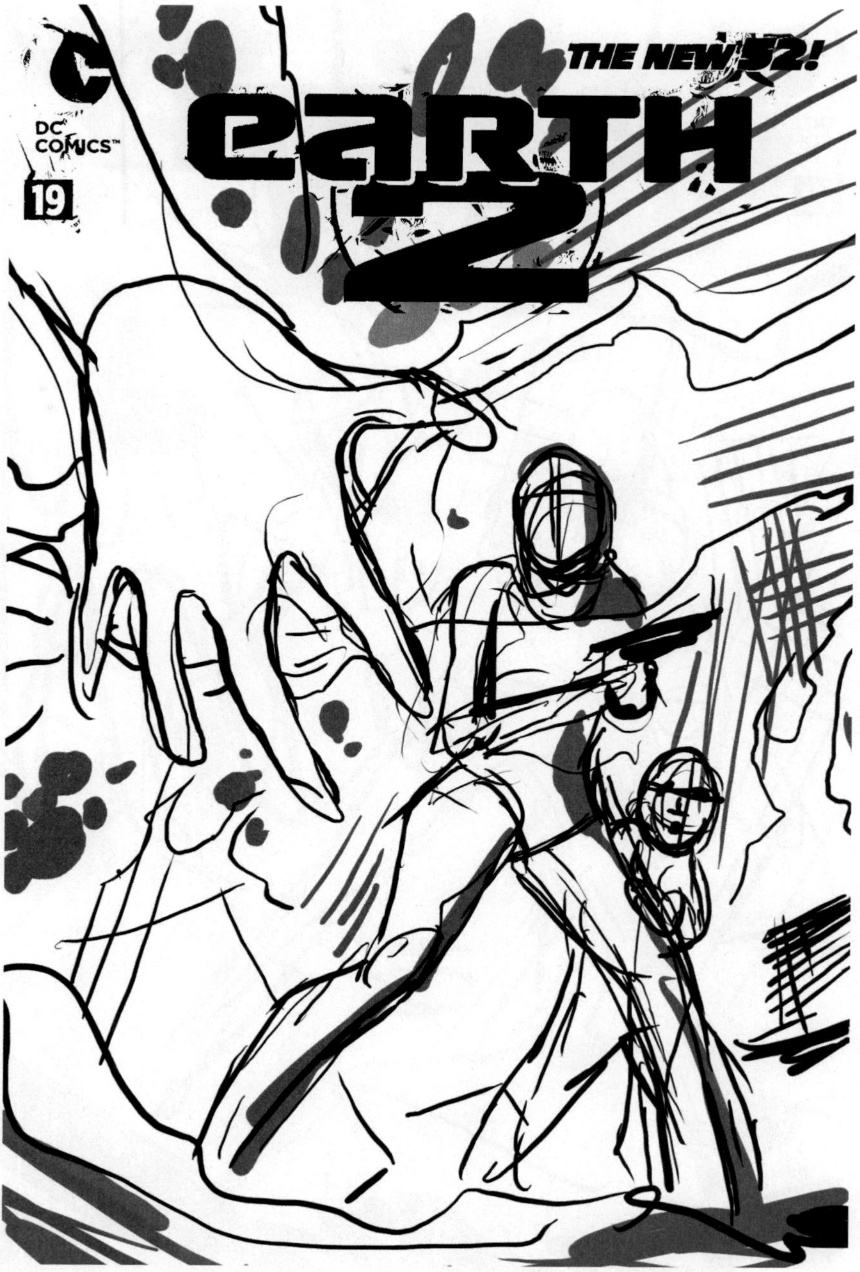
THE NEW 52!
DC COMICS™
19
EARTH 2

EARTH 2 #29 cover sketches
by Yildiray Cinar

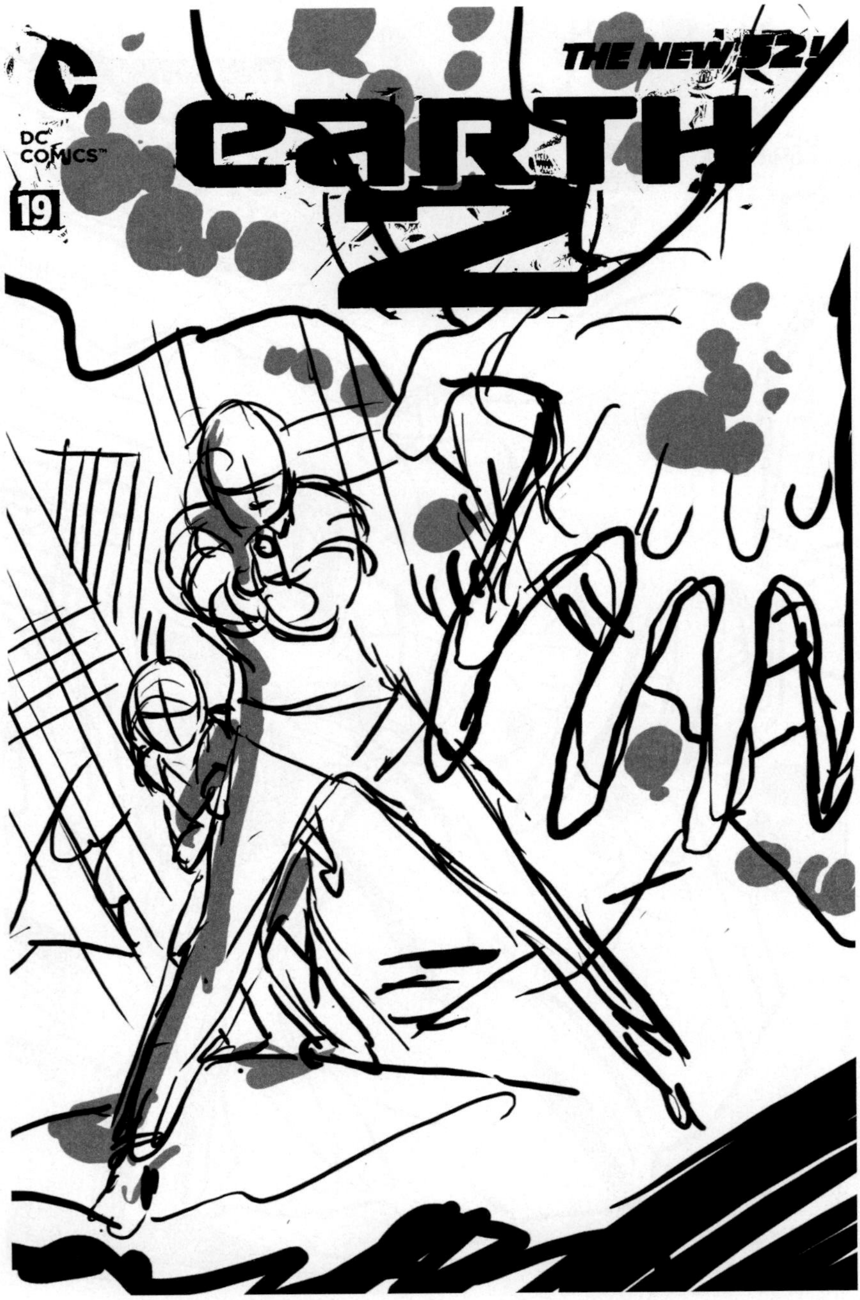
THE NEW 52!
DC COMICS
EARTH 2
19

START AT THE BEGINNING!
EARTH 2
VOLUME 1: THE GATHERING

EARTH 2 VOL. 2: THE TOWER OF FATE

with JAMES ROBINSON, NICOLA SCOTT and YILDIRAY CINAR

EARTH 2 VOL. 3: BATTLE CRY

with JAMES ROBINSON, NICOLA SCOTT and YILDIRAY CINAR

EARTH 2 VOL. 4: THE DARK AGE

with TOM TAYLOR and NICOLA SCOTT

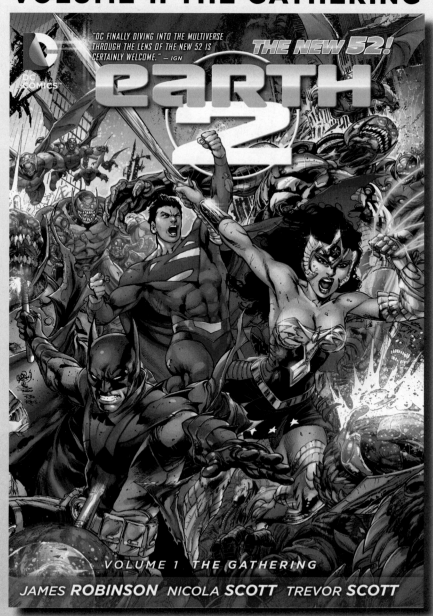

"DC FINALLY DIVING INTO THE MULTIVERSE THROUGH THE LENS OF THE NEW 52 IS CERTAINLY WELCOME." – IGN

THE NEW 52!

DC COMICS

EARTH 2

VOLUME 1 THE GATHERING

JAMES **ROBINSON** NICOLA **SCOTT** TREVOR **SCOTT**

START AT THE BEGINNING!
JUSTICE LEAGUE
VOLUME 1: ORIGIN
GEOFF JOHNS and JIM LEE